D0855955

WEALTHFULNESS

WEALTHFULNESS

Simple Steps to Financial

Health and Happiness

LANCE ALSTON

BROWN BOOKS
PUBLISHING GROUP

Wealthfulness: Simple Steps to Financial Health and Happiness

Publisher's Cataloging-In-Publication Data

Names: Alston, Lance.
Title: Wealthfulness : simple steps to financial health and happiness / Lance Alston.
Description: Dallas, Texas : Brown Books Publishing Group, [2018] | Includes bibliographical references.
Identifiers: ISBN 978-1-61254-869-2
Subjects: LCSH: Finance, Personal. | Wealth. | Well-being.
Classification: LCC HG179 .A47 2018 | DDC 332.024--dc23

Brown Books Publishing Group
16250 Knoll Trail Drive, Suite 205
Dallas, Texas 75248
www.BrownBooks.com
(972) 381-0009

A New Era in Publishing®

ISBN 978-1-61254-869-2
LCCN 2017939509

Printed in the United States
10 9 8 7 6 5 4 3 2 1

For more information or to contact the author, please go to www.Wealthfulness.com.

I dedicate this book to my parents, who watched with patience and encouragement as I chose roads less traveled; to my brothers—Daryn, whom I will miss the rest of my life, and Chris, because you are uniquely you; and to Claire and Olivia. My precious girls, you represent my greatest joys today and my brightest hopes for tomorrow.

Contents

Acknowledgments

The original draft for this book was written in the mountains of New Mexico over the course of several years. Few words from that early manuscript found their way onto these pages, for which I have my editor, Darla Bruno, to thank. Darla was given a difficult task yet somehow managed to draw a completely different—and far more useful—book from that first draft. Rewriting a book requires uncommon levels of commitment and patience from everyone involved, and Brown Books turned out to be the perfect publisher for this project. Milli Brown is a force of nature and the best cheerleader anyone could ever have on their team. Milli and Darla, thank you for your talent, for your professionalism, and for your kindness when this project became more challenging than anyone expected. Abigail Thrift, Katlin Stewart, and Hallie Raymond were essential in keeping this project on track and holding me accountable along the way.

Many of the ideas for this book sprouted from interviews I conducted between 2005 and 2008 with my former business partner and cohost, Jim Whiddon. Jim, you changed my life when you handed me that book on passive investing, exactly as you predicted. I will treasure my memories of those years as we grew the business and raised our families.

To this day, I am still awed by the fact that people like John Bogle, Scott Burns, and Burton Malkiel will answer a personal e-mail or phone call. Many busy people generously made time for our interviews over the years, and I thank each and every one of them. It was an honor and a privilege to be part of those conversations.

Barbara Saunders and Kathy Muldoon deserve special mention for their guidance early in my career. I wouldn't have made it without them. A handful of colleagues have shared their considerable personal and professional wisdom with me over the last two decades: Tom McIntire, Lyn McIntire, Patrick Dougherty, Jim Middlebrook, Trudy Turner, Harvey Matte, Brent Little, and John Gay. I am a better financial planner and a better person because of your friendships. My high school English teacher, Doris Wolff, introduced me to Henry David Thoreau and dared me to live the life I had imagined. Every kid deserves a teacher like Doris in his or her life.

Thanks also to the volunteers who read various versions of this book: Patrick Dougherty, Margaret O'Day,

Bob Purcell, Carol Purcell, Sharon Johnson, Amy Rogers, and my mom, Sue Alston. This book benefited from your literary insights and keen eyes for detail. Alesha Isaacs jumped in at the eleventh hour to help get the book print ready—Alesha, you were awesome. Tona Bell, owner of The Paper Seahorse, was a joy to work with as we searched for a special image to go in the book.

A book, as any writer will tell you, is one of those projects resembling an iceberg: the bulk of it lies hidden below the waterline, invisible to a casual observer on the surface. There simply would be no book without the constant support and collaboration of my business partner, Tiffany Finney-Johnson. Tiffany, you are one of the most talented and intellectually curious individuals I know; however, it's your heart that makes you special. No amount of training can teach someone to care about our clients the way you do. Thank you for making our firm what it is. Thanks also to Ryan Johnson, your husband, for the interesting questions and humor he regularly adds to our work day. Harper and Cole, your parents are wonderful people!

To my brother Chris, for keeping it interesting and fun all these years. You have always challenged me to become better. Thank you. I hope you find your personal ikigai, because you have so much to offer this world. I only wish our brother Daryn were here to share this part of the journey with us. Our parents, Dick and Sue Alston, have created an amazing community of family and friends during their life together. They embody the central idea of this book—a life well lived, filled with happiness, friends, and success. Mom and Dad, thank you for your wisdom, values, and unconditional love.

And finally, to my girls, Claire and Olivia, who have put up with this book in our house for a very long time. You give my life joy and meaning, and it is for you two precious daughters that I write.

Preface

Before we begin, I would like to offer you—my reader—an interesting concept to keep in mind as you read through this book. Dr. Atul Gawande is a bestselling author and a regular contributor to the *New Yorker* magazine. When he's not writing, Dr. Gawande is a full-time surgeon at one of Boston's most prestigious hospitals. In a recent article he discussed a fundamental challenge confronting modern medicine, one that I believe applies to personal financial planning as well.

As a surgeon, Dr. Gawande's primary job is to intervene in someone's health care when there is a problem. If the intervention goes well, a problem is solved, and everyone moves on with their lives. This is how we view the practice of medicine—get sick, go to the doctor, get cured. And yet, as he points out, most of the ways we can become and remain healthy require slow, incremental changes to our bodies' systems. We do not lose weight, lower our blood pressure, or improve our cholesterol quickly or effortlessly. Committed care, where doctor and patient act as a team, provides the best path for sustained health; however, this kind of process takes much more time and effort than the interventionist approach.

The contrast is between an immediate, heroic intervention and a tedious, incremental rate of change. Interventionism or incrementalism? We all, of course, get more excited about the quick fix, but many important improvements in life don't respond well to grand interventions. In this respect, I believe personal financial planning is a lot like the practice of medicine. Consumers often look to the financial industry for a quick fix so they can get back to their busy lives. They're looking for someone to put their inheritance to work, fix their portfolio, or tell them it's okay to retire.

This book is my attempt to disrupt that prevailing interventionist mind-set when it comes to personal finance. I am proposing a better approach—incremental change, with regular, mindful effort. I believe this alternative paradigm will empower you to take control of your finances and greatly improve your financial future. I'm not offering revolutionary new ideas, just a healthy dose of common sense and personal experience.

"Success, therefore, is not about the episodic, momentary victories, though they do play a role. It is about the longer view of incremental steps that produce sustained progress."

—*Atul Gawande*[1]

Let's get started.

Introduction

It starts for most people with a barely perceptible unease. Maybe you just turned fifty or had a baby or took a big promotion. Whatever it was, something changed, and now you sense that your financial world is suffering from inattention. But you really don't have the time to tackle those financial issues, so you put your concerns in the back of your mind and try to forget about them.

You might be worrying you haven't prepared enough for retirement. Maybe it bothers you that you don't have a will or enough life insurance or you're spending way too much. These worries are left to roam your subconscious, taking up valuable energy and time—two things you can't afford to waste.

We are all busier than ever, and we have countless gadgets to monopolize our attention, along with plenty of ways to spend our hard-earned cash. We experience hundreds of encounters each day where someone is selling us something—trying to evoke our natural instincts to focus more on today than on the future. Each one of those encounters taxes our brains, causing it to fire off neurons to make a calculation, a decision, or a mental note. The bad news is we are terrible as a species at delaying gratification, and those advertisers trying to sell us stuff know our weaknesses. We are simply no match for their marketing expertise and resources.

Our fast-paced consumer lifestyles are constantly testing the limits of our mental capacity. We can't possibly remember everything that needs to be done in a day, and there's no chance of getting it all checked off. So the planner in us begins to make lists of things to do, groceries to buy, and people to call. Then there are the vacation lists, work lists, party lists, kid lists. You get the point; the planner in our head stays very busy.

It doesn't matter whether the lists are kept in a book, on your phone, or in your head; they are all taxing what psychologists call your mental bandwidth. And one of the most important items on your lists, whether you realize it or not, is money. Thoughts about money and financial issues tax your mental bandwidth like almost nothing else.

From new areas of research in psychology and economics, we are learning that worrying about money can interfere with a person's focus and basic problem-solving skills. In fact, chronic money worries have been shown to lower mental processing ability enough to drop your IQ roughly thirteen points. That's a lot. By some estimates, that's enough to move a person from the category of superior IQ to average, or worse, from average to borderline deficient.[1] Ouch.

You can go on for years curating your financial to-do lists, planning for that free weekend when you'll get those things checked off. The list will get longer, though, and it will surely feel overwhelming at times. It's also unlikely that list will ever get prioritized, which can lead to spending far too much time on the insignificant things. Would it surprise you to know most families spend more time each year planning their vacation than they do planning for their retirement or college?

Unlike any previous time in history, our challenge in the modern world is not too little, but rather too much. We have too many choices, too many distractions, too many things, people, and places vying for our attention. The fundamental problem we face is prioritization.

President Dwight Eisenhower is credited with a framework for tackling the problem of prioritizing the many things you want to get done. Considering he orchestrated the Allied invasion of France during World War II, I assume he thought quite a bit about priorities. In Eisenhower's view, there are two ways to define any problem—those that are urgent and those that are important. For most of us, the urgent problems tend to tyrannize the important ones, and in the end we run out of time to address what's really important.

One example is retirement. The sad truth is most Americans enter retirement without giving much consideration to their financial future. Less than one-third of Baby Boomers over the age of fifty have ever attempted to create a financial plan, and only about 20 percent feel confident they have a plan in place. The rest either never tried or gave up.[2]

Only one out of five people over fifty has a plan for their retirement. How is that possible?

This book is intended to be the first step in the process of changing your paradigm when it comes to personal finance. Why, you ask? Because the conventional approach to managing your finances simply does not work in the twenty-first century. I call this new paradigm Wealthfulness—a thoughtful approach to life that gives equal weight to your money and your happiness.

In chapter 1 I will challenge you to stop for a moment and give some consideration to your financial world. Becoming mindful of your current condition and your future goals is a necessary first step if you want to permanently change your existing paradigm. I'm not suggesting this will be easy; however, your financial future deserves some undivided attention from time to time.

Chapter 2 questions the conventional approach to investing you're probably accustomed to. Your investments are rarely the most important piece of your financial world, but you have to get your portfolio right before we move on to anything else. I'll start with a few questions to consider that may help you rethink your portfolio and your attitude about investing.

It doesn't matter whether you have a million-dollar portfolio or you're just starting your first 401(k) account; the standard stock-broker approach to investing is wasting a large portion of YOUR money. That old Wall Street investing paradigm has been failing investors for decades, and a change for the better is long overdue. Is there an easier and more effective way to manage your portfolio? In fact, there is, and just about every single person in the industry knows it.

Changing your investment paradigm can simplify your life and empower you to start planning for and realizing your lifelong financial goals. How, what, and why—these are the important questions you should be asking about your portfolio before you ever invest one dime. You need to get the investing part right in the beginning, but then it should take up very little of your time for the rest of your life. Yes, you read that last sentence correctly—*for the rest of your life.*

Like many people nowadays, you may not completely trust the financial industry or get excited about handing your money to them. Over the last few decades the big banks and Wall Street firms have lost most of the public's trust—something we'll talk about when we look at the psychology of money from the perspective of behavioral finance in chapter 3.

Behavioral finance is a relatively new area of study that bridges the gap between economics and psychology. For decades, economists have been uncovering a long list of examples where people seem to make the same mental mistakes repeatedly. It turns out these behavioral finance mistakes have a lot to teach us when it comes to managing the family finances, and we are now beginning to understand why taking charge of your personal finances can be daunting for so many people. Cognitive biases like overconfidence, risk aversion, and a selective memory are all working against your financial plan. Understanding those behavioral biases will help you make better financial decisions and worry less.

I've spent almost twenty years helping families manage their personal finances. Along the way I've met with just about every possible personality type across four generations, and I can tell you they all had a unique vision for their financial future. Each individual also brought with them an emotional connection to the money required to pay for that future. Your past experiences, your emotions, and your happiness are all connected to money in some fashion.

However, your happiness will never be just about dollar signs, and that's what we'll talk about in chapter 4: rethinking the connection between your money and happiness. Remember, our goal is to integrate a thoughtful perspective on your wealth with a proactive attitude about your goals, dreams, and ultimate happiness. Wealthfulness requires you to ask what you want your financial future to look like. This is much more difficult to quantify than your salary or your net worth, but it matters a lot.

All the planning in the world won't lead to an improvement in your financial life if you don't eventually take action. Good intentions will not be enough. The ideas we cover in chapter 5 are intended to help you get started on your personal financial journey. We'll talk about staying on track with feedback loops and building your financial world in ways that "nudge" you into better choices. Again, these ideas and others we cover in chapter 5 come from new areas of research in behavioral finance, and they are available to anyone who wants to take charge of their world. Very soon you'll be ready to embark on your personal path toward Wealthfulness.

Please don't worry that your world is about to become a lot more complicated. It is just the opposite. The ultimate goal of this book is to help you simplify your financial life and worry less. If that sounds like something you're interested in, this book can help you get there.

I wrote this book to help you get started working toward those goals. Here are the five simple steps we'll cover:

1. Bring purpose and intention to your financial future.
2. Fix your portfolio for good by answering a few questions.
3. Recognize and avoid the behavioral biases and mistakes that can derail your financial plan.
4. Reconsider the personal connection between your money and happiness.
5. Apply some simple concepts from behavioral finance that will help you get started and stay on track with our financial plan.

These steps can unleash the energy, time, and mental bandwidth you've spent on worrying for so many years. Remember, the goal of Wealthfulness is not simply more money, it's a fulfilling life with more meaning and happiness.

Before we begin, let me share a few sobering statistics on the current financial health of American households in general:

- More than 50 percent of all US households are at risk of not maintaining their current lifestyle in retirement.[3]
- 75 percent of all single retirees depend on social security for at least half of their income (50 percent of all married retirees).[4]
- Seven out of ten Americans own a credit card, and over half of those carry a balance.[5] The average is almost $16,000.[6]
- Americans now owe more in student loans than they do in credit card debt and auto loans.[7]
- Only 28 percent of Americans have enough emergency savings to cover six months of expenses.[8]
- One out of five households with kids younger than age eighteen has no life insurance.[9]

- According to a Federal Reserve study, the average household wealth in 2013 was only slightly higher than the level of wealth in 2001 after adjusting for inflation.[10]

- The 2013 Survey of Stress, published annually by the American Psychological Association, reported finding that 71 percent of survey respondents said they were stressed about money; 69 percent said they were stressed about work; and 59 percent said they were worried about the economy.[11]

The message seems quite clear: families today are doing a poor job of financial planning, whether it relates to college, retirement, health care, or providing for their family when the main breadwinner is gone. And yet Wall Street continues to offer only excitement and empty promises. What you really need is a new financial paradigm—a better way to invest, an understanding of your behavioral biases, and a path toward happiness in your life: Wealthfulness.

One final note—this book is not intended to give you quick answers to your financial questions. You won't find user-friendly checklists or "how-to" discussions about common financial problems at the end of each chapter. There are thousands of "how-to" financial books on

Amazon and thousands more promising ways to help you become some style of millionaire. To be more precise, I found 3,508 books with "millionaire" in the title when I searched business and finance books on Amazon. Some of those books are exceptional, and many are worth looking into; however, teaching you how to become a millionaire is not my objective for this book. We will leave the "how-tos" and millionaire game plans for those other books. I have included a recommended reading list in the appendix.

What I want to focus on, instead, is the incremental changes that can lead to long-term financial health, and for that you need a new way of thinking about your finances. You need to break free from conventional thinking when it comes to the financial industry, investing, and your role in the process.

As Steven Covey points out in his book *7 Habits of Highly Effective People*, you have to begin with the right mind-set if you intend to make real changes in your life.[12] Wealthfulness is that kind of mind-set.

1

Money and Mindfulness: Be Mindful of Your Financial World

"…as you get older you become the person you always should have been."

—*David Bowie[1]*

Make no mistake, the concept of retirement is experiencing profound changes. Baby boomers are retiring at a rate of ten thousand each day, and this trend will continue for more than a decade. As they enter the next chapter in their lives, boomers face a retirement landscape entirely different from the generations before them. Employers no longer offer pension plans, the Social Security system is unstable, health-care costs continue to rise, and any possible inheritance is being depleted as their parents live longer.

That popular image of retirement as a carefree twilight spent with family and friends on the porch no longer exists. In fact, it probably never did.

As I mentioned in the introduction, personal financial planning is about much more than just investing. You should start with a clear picture of your current financial situation and then combine that reality with your long-term goals and dreams. In essence, you are working toward a more complete understanding of both your present and your future. Yet too many people lack the tools or awareness to look beyond the present.

As a financial planner, I help clients wrestle with this challenge of balancing the present and the future every day. I generally meet with three types of people in my practice—one group simply ignores their financial problems out of fear; others constantly worry they haven't done enough; while some actually enjoy financial planning and feel pretty good about their situation. That last group is quite small, and oftentimes they're missing important pieces.

If you belong to the first group, the ones who are terrified to take a comprehensive look at their financial situation, I promise it's not nearly as difficult or as painful as you imagine. And the sooner you start, the better. On the other hand, if you have a financial plan, but you're still worrying way too much, then maybe all you need is a little coaching to help you get moving. People who find themselves in group two generally already know what they need to do yet still can't seem to get their financial life in order.

What if you don't recognize yourself in group one or two? You just might belong to that rare third group we call the overachievers. For this bunch, money has always held great importance, and they treat it with special attention. They budget and save, get the right amount of insurance, keep an eye on their taxes, and have wills that are actually signed. (You'd be surprised how many aren't.)

The overachievers watch their finances closely. And they count. And compare. How much did they have at thirty? At forty? How much will they have at retirement? How much do their friends have? How can they get more sooner?

Are you scared and confused like group one, frustrated like group two, or maybe obsessed with your finances like group three? Tragically, the overachievers with million-dollar portfolios are often no happier or less anxious than the people in group one doing nothing. Why? Because the underlying question causing their anxiety hasn't been addressed: Am I going to be okay? Having more and more and more will never answer that question until you start to think about your personal definition of "okay."

You're probably thinking right now how crazy that sounds—someone has millions of dollars, and they're still stressed about their lives? Yes, based on my experience, those millionaires are quite often just as anxious as the next person. Take Jim and his wife Carol, for instance.

Jim started working in sales when he was seventeen. He had always been goal driven, finding success wherever he landed. By his mid-twenties he was saving a large part of his income and he had a very clear plan to have $1 million in the bank before he turned forty. That goal evolved over time into a target of several million dollars when he reached fifty and retired.

Every December, Jim would track his progress with an elaborate spreadsheet. Most years he exceeded his goals, but when he didn't, he worked extra hard the next year to catch up. Jim and Carol came to us when they were both forty-three and well on their way to successfully retiring at fifty.

Each year we would meet to discuss their financial plan, and each year Jim would bring his spreadsheet for us all to review. There on the spreadsheet, in the row next to the year Jim turned fifty, was the word "RETIRE" in

capital letters. We'll talk more about that heavy word—
RETIRE—later in the book.*

Our fourth annual meeting, when the couple was
forty-six, started off a bit differently than the previous
ones. Usually, we would get right to work discussing his
business and reviewing the progress toward their retirement goal, which was now only four years away. "I've seen
three changes in my life since we last met, and I hold you
responsible," he said to start the meeting this time. "I've
gained ten pounds; bought a new car, which I've never
done before; and started working less."

Not knowing where this discussion was leading, I
hesitated before saying anything.

"Okay. That's interesting. How do you feel about those
changes?" I asked. As I said it, I had that old legal adage
swirling around in my mind—don't ask a question if you
don't know the answer. I braced myself for the answer.

"I feel great," Jim responded as Carol shook her head
in agreement.

---

* The concept of retirement is becoming increasingly disconnected
from our modern economy and life expectancies. Many people are
working well beyond age sixty, or even seventy, because they enjoy
what they're doing and want to stay engaged. In chapter 4 we talk
about the connection between money and happiness.

"He's a different person," she added.

We spent the next two hours talking about what had occurred that year to change his mind-set so dramatically. In his words, Jim felt like he could "finally take my foot off the accelerator." Things were going just fine, and after three years of reviewing a financial plan that lasted until his ninety-fifth birthday, instead of looking at a spreadsheet that stopped at his fiftieth, he had finally accepted an obvious fact—they were okay.

That was something Jim and Carol had never considered before. In fact, neither one of them had ever talked about why they were trying so hard to save or why he wanted to retire at fifty. It was just a goal Jim set for himself long ago—before the kids and a job he enjoyed.

Jim had gained ten pounds because he loved to cook and entertain, something they were now doing much more often. I doubt anyone wants to learn that a successful financial plan will add ten pounds to your other bottom line, but don't worry. Remember, we're talking about incremental changes, which often lead to other changes over time. Jim was already talking about joining a local gym now that he had more free time on his hands.

He was working less because he had hired several people to help him expand his company into new cities. The change in mind-set had allowed him to see his business in a different, more creative light. That's what happens when you write down your goals and track your progress—it reduces your anxiety and unleashes your creativity. That is something we'll talk more about in chapter 5.

As for the new car, he loved it.

Without the thoughtful, incremental process of financial planning, Jim and Carol would have carried on as they had the previous twenty years. They would be striving for an arbitrary, outdated goal that was no longer relevant for their lives. Nothing had changed, except their definitions of success and purpose. Their mind-set.

Giving anything or anyone your undivided attention has become an uncommon luxury in our fast-paced world, but that is exactly what I'm going to ask you to do: give your financial situation the attention it deserves. You needn't be afraid, worried, or consumed by your financial issues, but you do need to commit the time and effort to understand your future goals and purpose. Like Jim and Carol, you will find the process prepares you to see your future differently.

In Eastern philosophy there is the concept of mindfulness—an ability to focus intently on your present condition or experience. Over the last few decades this

Eastern concept of focus or attention has found applications in Western medicine, psychology, and economics, just to name a few areas. The conclusions from Western science and Eastern philosophy agree: an ability to focus your attention helps reduce your overall stress and improves how you manage stressful situations.

In his book *The Mayo Clinc Guide to Stress Free Living*, Dr. Amit Sood explains:

> Stress is the struggle with what is. A mind that doesn't have what it wants or doesn't want what it has experiences stress . . . Understanding and working with the brain's and the mind's imperfections isn't a luxury; it is an absolute necessity if we hope to survive and thrive as a species.[2]

What do you have, and what do you want in life? Finding a stress-free balance between the two is one of the essential goals of any financial plan. But finding this balance is easier said than done. Dr. Sood warns us what we're up against: your brain and mind are hardwired to keep you stressed, constantly distracted from the present moment by impulses, infatuations, and fears.[3]

Remove Those Roadblocks

Researchers are beginning to understand exactly why we repeatedly make the same mistakes, and it's clear the average person is not as rational as economists like to think. Some of those biological adaptations that worked great in the forest aren't so useful when it comes to long-term planning for the future. Our ancestors' lives just weren't that long. We now have much longer futures to plan for, and our emotions and short-term preferences often interfere with what might be best for us in the long run.

In his book *The Happiness Hypothesis,* psychologist Jonathan Haidt uses the story of a rider (the planner) and an elephant (emotion) to explain how our brains work. Yes, the rider may have the reins, but which animal is really in control of the journey? That elephant doesn't have to go anywhere he doesn't want to go.[4]

It might surprise you to know the planner voice in your head—that guy or girl keeping everything organized with all of the lists—never gets anything done. It's the other voice—the guy or girl who *wants* something—that makes things happen. Have you ever tried for years to do something hard, like getting rid of debt or losing weight, with no long-term success to show for it? Then one day you just wanted it, and the rest is history. Professor Haidt's research shows us that motivation comes from our emotions, not our intellect.

Each of us has a rider in our head with lots of plans and lists. He thinks he's in control, but we also have an elephant to manage, and he has lots of wants and fears. You need to understand both animals in order to change your paradigm and expand your financial possibilities. People rarely take the time—purposefully make the time—to discuss their hopes and dreams and then make plans for achieving them. Sure, we all hope to retire someday, and we think occasionally of that incredible vacation of our dreams, but hope and daydreams won't help us reach our goals.

The greatest challenge for your logical side is managing the relentless tyranny of the urgent. We all know that getting your car washed, for example, is less important than having enough life insurance, but somehow the car gets taken care of and the life insurance doesn't.

This kind of procrastination comes in many shapes and sizes in the financial world. I often see couples whose wills were neglected for decades and then hurriedly drafted days before a trip out of the country. I also meet with people who, after months of avoiding the inevitable, must make a decision about a pension or early retirement with only days to consider their options. These aren't the kinds of issues to be tackled at the last minute, and yet they very often are.

I mentioned President Eisenhower in the introduction because he is credited with a framework for prioritizing the incessant stream of things to be done. It is presented below as a simple grid you may recognize:

	URGENT	NOT URGENT
IMPORTANT		
NOT IMPORTANT		

The process of purposely giving your full attention to your unique financial situation will help you sort out the things in your financial life that are unimportant or not urgent. From there you can set priorities and begin taking action based on importance rather than urgency. It has been estimated that an average brain is constantly occupied with approximately 150 items on its bucket list. Is it any wonder we modern Americans report being overwhelmed and stressed[5], or that money is our single biggest stressor?[6]

As Dr. Judson Brewer points out, it's the executive center of our brain—the prefrontal cortex—that goes offline first when we're stressed. His research into addictive behavior tells us what we can all attest to—stress leads to that pint of ice cream, cigarette, or Netflix binge we know isn't good for us.[7] So why do we do it? Because the executive control center (the rider) shuts down, leaving you to wrangle with your emotional, stressed-out elephant.

And like stress, too much information or too many choices can lead to the same problem with executive control. Your rider just can't handle the workload. We'll talk about choice overload and how it can paralyze you later in the book.

*"A wealth of information creates
a poverty of attention."*

—*Herbert Simon, Nobel Laureate, Economics*[8]

Get Ready for Change

Several years I ago, I watched a movie called *March of the Penguins* with my family. It is a marvelous documentary with breathtaking scenery, but for me the story was almost unbearable to watch.

The stars of the movie are a flock of emperor penguins facing immense challenges—they lay their eggs and incubate them through the Antarctic winter (not an easy thing to do); to avoid predators, they must nest far inland, many miles from their food source in the ocean, and, well, they're penguins. They can't fly.

The birds have met these challenges by adopting what economist Jeffrey Ely calls "perpetually suboptimal behavior" that makes little sense to an outside observer. The penguins march sixty miles inland, starving for many months while they incubate their single egg in subzero Antarctic temperatures, then eventually trek back to the ocean to eat again. These adaptations allow the penguins to survive, but with each evolutionary adaptation their existence has become increasingly more complex. In the words of Ely, they have become *kludged*.[9]

The idea of a "kludge" crops up in a wide range of areas like the military, software programming, and aerospace engineering—all fields that confront immense complexity in the face of limited time and resources. In such environments a new problem often gets a patch or a quick fix, because reengineering the entire system is simply out of the question at the time. Thus the embedded patches continue to accumulate, allowing the system to become increasingly unstable.

Likewise, many families have financial situations that are equally unstable. It's not that they strive for this outcome, but with each small decision or commitment the family financial system becomes slightly more complex and unworkable. It becomes kludged.

You start with a kid or two, add a house, then a new job, a move and a few bad investments, and there you find yourself—at the age of forty or fifty or sixty—with a whole bunch of financial stuff but not much confidence it's working for you. The logical side of your brain keeps making plans, creating lists, and trying to check things off. At the same time, the emotional side of your brain is coming up with more wants and more worries about the uncertainty of it all. The two sides are not working together; in fact, much of the time they work at odds with one another, and the conflict is wearing you out.

You need a way to focus both sides of your brain toward action, with a clear plan for the future, instead of putting patches on your present situation. The good news is, unlike those poor penguins, there's a lot you can do to simplify your financial world and get control of it all.

Your first step toward Wealthfulness is to stop for a moment and acknowledge your financial concerns; slow down long enough to realize there's a bigger picture with a longer-term horizon. You need a plan.

2

Money and Markets: There Is an Easier and Better Way to Invest

"Forget the needle, buy the haystack."

—*John Bogle[1]*

One observation I have made over the years is that most people avoid thinking about long-term financial planning until they have money to invest. Here's a typical example of how these conversations go. Walking with my daughter, Olivia, to school one morning, we passed a neighbor going in the same direction. She was pushing a stroller with one hand and holding her kindergartner's hand with the other. We struck up a conversation that somehow turned to financial planning.

"Do you think it makes sense to see a financial advisor since we don't have any money to invest right now?" she asked. My neighbor was now a stay-at-home mom, and I knew her husband had gone through several unplanned job changes.

"Yes," I answered. "Do you have a will?"

"No," she responded sheepishly. (The vast majority of people we meet with do not.)

"How about an emergency cash fund? Do you think you guys have enough life insurance?"

During our five-minute walk to school, my neighbor confirmed that her family was not financially prepared on any dimension. She and her husband were both smart and very aware of the areas that needed their attention. However, everything they should be taking care of was on hold because they "didn't have any money to invest."

Of course they should be addressing their financial issues, regardless of their current portfolio. Wall Street has created a dangerous mind-set where people think of investing instead of financial planning, because that's been the conventional Wall Street profit model for the past hundred years.

With changes in your age and health, many of your options may become much more expensive or no longer available when you finally get around to planning. It doesn't matter how old you are or how much money you have saved; the process of assessing your financial situation and planning for your future will get you started on the right track.

Just don't think of that track as if it has been set in stone. Your plan will evolve with every change in your life. Babies, houses, and health issues will require adjustments to your financial plan. As important as the planning is, it's just as important to reassess your situation regularly and give your financial situation the attention it deserves. Remember, a mind-set of Wealthfulness entails incremental steps toward improving your financial health, which includes much more than just your investments.

But as I said earlier, we have to start with the investing part and get that right before we move on to more important planning questions. Most investors, based on my experience, have no idea what their portfolio should look like. In fact, it's not even a question they ever get around to asking. Do you need international stocks? What kinds of bonds? Are you missing out if you don't have exotic things like hedge funds and private equity or gold or rental property?

Here are a few observations I've made over the years: most Americans overinvest in US stocks, nobody understands bonds, and investors can rarely explain why their portfolio looks the way it does. That's the bad news, but don't despair.

One of the essential messages you should take away from this book is the fact that investing is not nearly as important, or as exciting, as Wall Street wants you to believe. Investing should be boring and uncomplicated. Done correctly, investing should take up very little of your time. So let's start there—with investing—and put some of the myths and misguided ideas to rest straight away.

Many people spend far too much time worrying about their portfolio and then neglect their investments nonetheless. Ironically, they imagine their investment decisions are so important that they become paralyzed in fear of making a mistake. Yes, it is critically important to build your portfolio properly in the first place, but from then on it's pretty darn difficult to make an investing mistake that will harm your financial future.

I have to warn you, though, it might just take all of the fun and excitement out of investing if you get your portfolio right in the beginning. That's a good thing. Never, ever invest your retirement savings in something you're excited about. If you find yourself excited about an investment, I can guarantee it probably has far too much in common with Las Vegas casinos. You're probably making a bet, not an investment.

Real investing is *not* gambling, although many people have come to confuse the two. In most cases, the confusion stems from poor investments they made in the past that turned out far riskier than expected. The tech bust in the early 2000s and the financial crisis in 2008 were painful periods that left investors wondering if the Wall Street game was rigged against them.

There are plenty of bad actors—both individuals and companies—and you definitely should be wary. But capitalism is not a gamble, and global stock markets are the best way to invest in capitalism, if you still believe in it. I do. However, in order to build a lifelong portfolio, you have to focus clearly on the most important elements and learn to ignore the incessant noise of the Wall Street casino. That's not easy.

Ask Yourself Why You Own Stocks in the First Place

Years ago I met someone who had more or less given up on investing. Claire, a successful businesswoman in her own right, had grown up watching her father accumulate wealth as a corporate executive. Her father had always had stockbrokers, so when her own company started to grow, Claire hired one of those big brokerage firms her dad recommended. That was back in the 1980s.

I met Claire almost thirty years later, just after she finally sold that successful business of hers. She and her husband flew into town one spring afternoon to interview our firm. The meeting went well, and within a few hours they were headed back to the airport to fly home. As Claire was leaving our office, she turned and smiled. "You know, if I invest with you, the market will start going down immediately. It has happened that way my whole life. What you really should do—" she said, "—you should pay us to go away. Your other clients will thank you later."

We all laughed as they headed out the door. "We'll show her," I thought.

That was the spring of 2007, and Claire was right. We put her portfolio together in July of that year—she wouldn't see a gain in her accounts until 2010. None of us knew at the time the US housing bubble was bursting, along with all the toxic investments Wall Street firms had created on top of the real estate bubble. Trillions of dollars were lost in investments across the globe, while millions of people lost their jobs. Sure, the banks and brokerage firms paid billions of dollars in fines, but nobody at the top went to jail. The criminals of Wall Street rarely see jail time for their misdeeds.

Over the following three years, from 2007 to 2010, I learned a lot about Claire's investing history. Her advisors had come and gone at a rate of two or three each decade. They sold her tax shelters in the 80s that went bust with the Reagan tax reforms; put plenty of Enron shares in the portfolio right before that scandal made them worthless; added "exclusive" private equity deals during the biotech and oil phases, which all went south; and loaded her up on technology bets during the tech bust.

Claire had been very successful during her career, and she and her husband were excellent savers who lived well below their means. Unfortunately, much of their hard work ended up benefiting their advisors rather than their retirement portfolio. The problem was that all of their investing experience was really not investing at all—it was speculating. Betting with their hard-earned money that some advisor was going to make them a lot of money and losing most of the time.

For the first time in all those years of "investing," Claire finally had a portfolio that looked like a long-term investment, not a short-term bet. Together we watched the portfolio drop precipitously as the global economy spiraled into a major recession. Her life savings dropped almost 40 percent before it hit bottom. Along the way, we made a few small changes but basically left the portfolio alone during the worst bear market since the Great Depression.

Now almost ten years later, Claire and her husband understand long-term investing. They've weathered a severe market drop and seen what capital markets can accomplish when given time.

Don't think for a minute those three years were easy, though. There were many long phone calls to keep her spirits up, along with lots and lots of data on past bear markets like 1973–1974, 1987, and 2000–2002. She stayed invested (finally) because she had a financial plan that showed her retirement was still going to be okay. When you only look at the dollar amount on your statements, drops like 2008 can be terrifying. A financial plan can help you see farther out into the future and put the ups and downs in context.

Did you stick to your investing plan during 2008–2009? If not then, could you do it now that you know what followed? Although the world stock markets plunged 40 percent during the 2008 banking crisis, 2009 was one of the best years on record. You may still cringe when you hear about Claire's terrible ride because you had a similar experience, but remember, by 2010 you were back to even if you stayed the course. The tech bust in 2000, Black Monday 1987, and the '73–'74 oil embargo were all similar experiences in hindsight.

The truth is most people NEED riskier investments, like stocks, in order to retire with an acceptable lifestyle. You simply cannot reach your retirement spending goals with CDs and bonds. You need stocks.*

Let's look at an example. If you invested $10,000 each year of a thirty-year career, you could retire with a portfolio valued over $660,000 if it grew at 5 percent annually—a return close to the historical returns for a bond portfolio. On the other hand, if your money grew at a rate of 10 percent—the historical return for the S&P 500—you would have over $1,600,000, or almost $1 million more for retirement. We don't know if future stock returns will be closer to 5 percent or 10 percent, but we do know that

---

* The best way to invest in stocks is through a mutual fund or exchange traded fund (ETF). Most investors should try to minimize or eliminate the individual stocks in their portfolio. If you'd like to learn more about investing, you can find definitions, detailed explanations, and lots of other resources on my website: www.Wealthfulness.com/investing101.

stocks have historically had much higher long-term returns than bonds.

Stocks also have a lot more risk, as we all witnessed in 2008. But that extra risk you necessarily must accept with stocks is worth it for the extra return, if done properly. Risk and return are always connected. One million dollars would make a considerable difference in your retirement lifestyle, but you have to include stocks in your portfolio and be prepared when they lose value from time to time.

So here we are again, confronted by the conflict between the two sides of your brain—the rider and the elephant. Your analytical rider knows stock returns are necessary, but your emotional elephant is terrified of the risks. A clearly defined financial plan for your future can make the uncertainty manageable by giving you some context for the ups and downs you'll inevitably experience from stock markets.

Question: Should you own risky asset classes like US and international stocks in the first place? Are you prepared for a 5 percent or 10 percent or even 20 percent drop in your portfolio? Do you need all the risk you have in your portfolio to achieve your goals? What amount of risk should you have?

Choose a Better Way to Invest

By far the most important question you will face as an investor is "how" to invest, not "what" to invest in. Every investor, whether they have $1,000 or $1,000,000, should start by asking themselves a few simple questions: Do I believe it's possible to make better returns than the average investor? Am I smarter than the market?

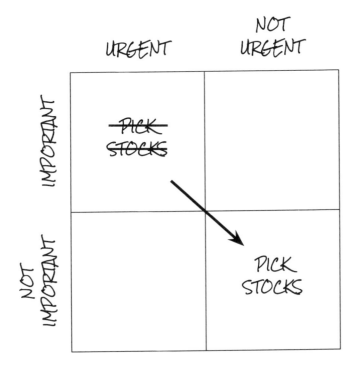

The conventional Wall Street approach to investing starts with a great new idea, some secret research or a looming trend that has yet to be recognized. Get the right new idea or spot the next big trend and you will get rich; that's the game. We call this approach *active investing*, and it's been Wall Street's empty promise for more than one hundred years.

Active investors behave exactly as their name implies—they actively buy and sell stocks based on some investing strategy. This type of investor is trying to beat the market with exceptional stock selection and by timing when they get in and out of their investments. Their goal is to get a return better than the average return they could get from buying and holding a large group of stocks, such as the S&P 500 Index. Simply put, active investors would rather not invest in all five hundred stocks in the index because they plan on buying only the good ones.

We would all love to buy only the winners, of course, but that doesn't seem to happen much in real life. Of the thousands of professionally managed mutual funds available to investors, most don't beat their part of the market in any given year. Take a longer view of five or ten years and you'll find that few mutual funds end up beating their index, i.e., they're not very successful at picking only the winning stocks.

Let me state this another way so that I'm perfectly clear. Most actively managed mutual funds are losers. Not surprisingly, this isn't a fact the mutual fund companies like to share with the public, because their profits depend on the eternal hope of beating those markets. There is another way to invest, however, if you suspect it's not that easy to pick only the winning stocks—follow the evidence.[**]

We now have over fifty years of compelling research from the fields of finance and economics to help you build the right portfolio. There is no secret, and the prescription is surprisingly simple. First of all, we know that diversification is one of the most important ingredients for a successful long-term portfolio, so you need to own different types of US and international stocks and bonds. Secondly, we also know that owning thousands of stocks and bonds is much safer than owning just a few. Finally, the cost of your investments is one of the most important ingredients in a successful investing plan. That's it:

[**] Terms such as evidence based investing, market return investing, or passive investing have much in common—their primary objective is to own thousands of stocks and bonds using low-cost mutual funds or exchange traded funds (ETFs). You can find more information on these investing concepts on my website: www.Wealthfulness.com/investing101.

1. Diversify by owning many different types of stocks and bonds—we call each type an asset class.
2. Use mutual funds or exchange traded funds to own lots of stocks and bonds instead of buying individual investments.
3. Keep the costs for your investments low.

These simple principles are based on academic research and five decades of evidence from real-life money managers. We'll call this type of approach *diversified market return investing*.

But what does market return investing look like? The goal is to own as much of the global stock markets as possible, intentionally accepting average returns, and earning year after year what the markets offer. Yes, average. Most people don't like settling for average, but here's the paradox: people are generally pretty close to average in most areas of their life. And half are below average. Likewise, most investors must get something close to an average return, and for every investor who beats the markets there is someone who loses.

Once you've decided to own as many stocks as possible rather than trying to select only the best, a wonderful thing happens—your cost of investing goes *way* down. You see, all that active investing is very expensive; you have to hire traders and analysts and fund managers, along with lots of marketing people to tell your exciting story. Most of those costs go away if you buy into the entire market with something like an index fund. Market return investing is not only great for diversification but also a very inexpensive way to invest.

There is one important caveat you must be aware of as a market return investor, though. Investors can make *a lot* more money through active investing than they ever could by owning the whole market. But can they do it consistently? Did I get your attention? Remember that investing should never be exciting, and if it is, there is probably some gambling going on.

Active investing begins with the assumption that the investor or the mutual fund manager or the financial advisor—someone—is smarter than the other participants in the markets. And if you can find that "special" person, or if that savant is you, then you'll be rewarded handsomely.

To repeat: In the short run you could potentially make much more money with active investing than you ever will with a market return portfolio. Unfortunately, investors can also lose much more with active investing. Just think of the bad news some stocks have experienced in the last few years—British Petroleum, Volkswagen, or Chipotle to name just a few. Could you stand to see your retirement accounts drop 50 percent from year to year? Probably not. Market return investors must to be willing to walk away from that siren's call of an investing home run, because it's simply not worth the risk.

Active investing requires a considerable amount of time, money, and stress for the POSSIBILITY of earning more money. In contrast, market return investing gives an investor the freedom to accept a reasonable portfolio return and stop worrying about markets. Remember, the goal of Wealthfulness is peace of mind and a successful financial future, not simply more money.

Years of actual mutual fund data prove that market return investing offers a much better chance at long-term success. This conclusion is confirmed by the steady stream of large institutions, like the $300 billion California pension fund for state employees, moving toward market return portfolios.[2] Famous investors such as Warren Buffett and David Swenson, along with former SEC Chairman Arthur Levitt, have all added their vocal support to the trend toward market return investing. Basically, everyone is adopting market return portfolios except the brokers who make their money working with average investors like you.

Hundreds of billions of dollars are moving out of Wall Street's conventional gambling games each year and into more reasonable long-term investing strategies. Investing based on evidence and scientific research, not hype.

Several years ago two economists, Diane Del Guercio and Jonathan Reuter, published a research paper on this passive-versus-active-investing question. They looked at the most popular mutual funds used by stockbrokers working for the big banks and brokerage firms and found that the broker-sold funds made up almost half of all mutual funds available in the United States during the period they studied. Del Guercio and Reuter concluded that the popular funds sold by brokers *underperformed* comparable index funds by 1.12 percent annually.[3]

More than 1 percent per year in lost return.

And these brokers were getting paid by their clients for this bad advice. Even worse, the researchers saw little trend over the eight years they studied toward the better-performing index funds. The percentage of broker-sold index funds increased only slightly—from 0.33 percent to 2.1 percent.

In the conclusion of their paper, Del Guercio and Reuter suggested two possible reasons for this unacceptable outcome:

1. **Unsophisticated clients** who didn't know what to ask for.
2. A broker environment with **no incentives to provide better investing choices** for those clients.

That research paper was published several years before the real estate bubble collapsed. More recent research tells us advisors' behavior hasn't changed much at all since the 2008 financial crisis. A separate study conducted in 2012 found similar results, noting in the conclusion, "Advisers encourage returns-chasing behavior and push for actively managed funds that have higher fees, even if the client starts with a well-diversified, low-fee portfolio."[4] Sadly, investors continue to be brainwashed to expect research reports and seminars and manager changes in their expensive funds instead of a simple market return approach.

Question: How is your portfolio invested? Do you spend hours on investment research, wondering whether to buy or sell, questioning your last trade, or searching for your next one? Are you meeting regularly with your financial advisor to discuss changes to your team of money managers because of poor performance?

Is this really the best use of the limited time you have to spend on much larger priorities like your family, friends, and work? Especially considering your investing efforts probably won't make much difference in the long run, and they're likely to make matters worse.

Accept What the Markets Give You

One of the most dangerous misconceptions in the investing game is the belief that there is someone out there who can make you money. It doesn't matter whether you're investing yourself or using an advisor, it's still a loser's game when you're trying to beat the market. Advisors can't make you money, but markets can.

In the short run plenty of investors, professional and amateur, can be wildly successful—but so can gamblers and lottery winners. In the long run, however, the only outcome you should expect from trying to beat the market is a lower return, i.e., less money.

Why? Because all of the activity from trying to beat the market adds layers of extra fees—expensive mutual funds, excessive trading costs, and higher advisor fees will all effectively reduce the return of your portfolio. It is always possible to have a negative effect on a portfolio return—just add more fees and trading costs to eat away at the readily available market return.

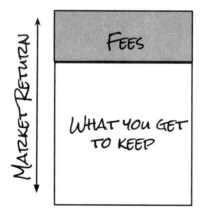

Many years ago, a successful Wall Street money manager named Charles Ellis came up with an analogy to describe the investing game. He suggested thinking of investing as if it were a tennis match. When you watch professional tennis you will probably notice the players make very few unforced errors. Tennis professionals don't make many mistakes, and it usually takes a winning shot to earn a point. In contrast, when you watch an amateur like me play tennis, the number of unforced errors goes up dramatically. We amateurs end up beating ourselves most of the time.[5]

Here's Ellis's point—the global markets make very few errors. With thousands of professional traders making over sixty million trades each day, there is no logical reason for you (or your advisor) to think you could outsmart the combined wisdom of the market. So what's a person to do if they can't beat the market? The best approach is to just keep up with the market, making as few "unforced" errors as possible.

> *Remember, in the long run, you*
> *or your advisor can't make you*
> *money; only the markets can.*

Each part of the market will earn a return over any particular time period you choose to measure. In the investing world we call the different parts of the market as-set classes. Every asset class—large or small stocks, growth or value stocks, US or international, various bonds, real estate—behaves differently from year to year.

Think of the returns for the various asset classes as the speed limits of capitalism. Take the five-year US Treasury Bond for instance; it's a boring bond issued by the US government, and it represents a very safe investment cat-egory. This asset class went up 13 percent in 2008 during the banking crisis as global investors rushed to safety. In contrast, just about every part of the US stock markets lost between 30 and 40 percent that year, and international markets were slightly worse.

It was a terrible year for stocks around the world—the worst year since the Great Depression—but short of get-ting out of the market completely, there was really nothing you or your advisor could do.

The next year, 2009, saw those same equity asset class-es go up between 30 and 80 percent. That year, too, your advisor had no control over those numbers. If you had simply ignored the markets and your portfolio from 2007 to 2010 you would have had no idea there had been a crash. That's what markets do—they go up, they go down, they recover. The goal should be not to control the process but rather to understand and plan for the inevitable volatility and extra return we get from stocks. Particularly if you're retired and living off of your portfolio, you should have a plan in place that recognizes the risks and returns.

And just to be clear, planning to get out of the markets in time to avoid a drop is a fool's game. In the years since the great banking crisis of 2008, I have not met one single person who got out in time to avoid the crash and got back into the markets in time to earn those exceptional 2009 returns. Successful market timers have a lot in common with Bigfoot—there are wildly popular stories of a sighting but very little evidence of their existence.

So what should you do? Market return investors need to decide how much of each asset class to put in their portfolio; for example, more bonds will slow the portfolio down, and more emerging markets stocks will speed it up—but remember, adding more emerging markets means a portfolio will go faster in both directions, up and down. All of the asset classes belong in your portfolio—all of the time. You do not get to pick and choose when each piece is added to the portfolio.

Think of Treasury bonds as your neighborhood school zone; S&P 500 stocks are like a city street; small stocks compare to the highways; and emerging markets act like a high-speed toll road. Each part of your portfolio has a different purpose and a different speed limit for any time you choose to measure it. Unfortunately for investors, the speed limits aren't posted in advance. We just have to live with these limits, all the while judiciously weighing the risks and rewards of each type of investment. You wouldn't build a city without all of the different types of roads, and you shouldn't build a portfolio without all of the different types of asset classes.

An advisor can help you do that, but he or she can't do anything about those returns. So stop listening to all of those great stock tips, and stop watching the markets.

Question: What do you expect from your investments? Do you honestly think you have any control over the returns in your portfolio? And do you believe there is a person or idea able to outwit the combined wisdom of the markets? Can you be happy (and successful) with the returns the market gives you?

Let me summarize quickly what we've covered in this chapter. The conventional approach to investing offered by the big banks and brokerage firms hasn't worked for decades, and it's not going to suddenly start working again. Actively buying and selling investments is not how global pension plans and foundations approach most of their investing, and it's definitely not the trend for smart individual investors either. Here's what you should be looking for instead, according to one team of researchers:

> We define 'good advice' as advice that moves the investor toward a low-cost, diversified, index-fund approach, which many textbook analyses on mutual fund investments suggest . . .[6]

You don't need a secret formula or special strategy, you simply need to accept the idea that characteristics like simple, low cost, and easy to understand are good things in the investing world. Jane Bryant Quinn, a well-known financial journalist who worked at *Newsweek* for thirty years, has a simple rule of thumb that works every time: don't invest in anything you can't explain to a fifth grader.[7]

In my experience this is the point in the investing story when many people start to question the whole passive investing idea. For some reason, the simplicity of owning as much of the global markets as possible causes many people to question the entire premise. I recall one potential client who got up to leave our first meeting rather abruptly, looking almost like she was upset or not feeling well. Then she quickly pivoted, sat back down in her chair, and said, "Why haven't I heard this before? My father is an engineer, and he's been investing for fifty years. My sister is the CFO of her company. But I've never heard anything like this from them. Why, why have I never heard of this before?"

I didn't have a good answer at the time, so I said offhandedly, "Because you weren't listening to the right people." Was that a bit harsh? Maybe. But it's my standard answer now.

To be honest, I still don't have a great answer for why most people keep giving their money to Wall Street. I just don't know. I've interviewed Eugene Fama, John Bogle,

Scott Burns, William Bernstein, Ken French—the brightest lights in the financial world—and their answers to that question are always just a little disappointing.

I can't tell you why fifty years of compelling evidence has yet to change the investing paradigm for most consumers. However, I can share a brief conversation I had with one of those luminaries, John Bogle. In the summer of 2009 I visited with Mr. Bogle in his office on the beautiful Vanguard campus in eastern Pennsylvania. We discussed the state of the industry post-2008, both the good and the bad changes that might come out of the global recession we had just experienced.

There was one point in the conversation I'll never forget. We were talking about low fees, transparency, and holding mutual fund directors accountable to the shareholders—the core ideas John Bogle built Vanguard on and the kind of changes we both hoped the industry would embrace after the crisis. He looked at me seriously and said, "I don't know anybody within the industry who believes what I'm doing is right."

"Really?" I asked. "Even if you talked to them one on one, they wouldn't see the value?"

John Bogle, a visionary who changed the face of investing with his indexing revolution, just shook his head no. I'm not sure that moment was at all sad for him, but it was for me.

"Lonely, sure, it feels lonely at times. I kind of like the lonely part," he laughed.

Don't be fooled by the industry advertising and hype. Those financial conglomerates have no intention of making investing easy or less expensive. You, however, have the power and the knowledge to make those changes personally in your portfolio.

Giving some thought to the basic questions at the foundation of your investing process will help reduce the time and worrying you spend on your finances. If you decide to follow the evidence and ignore Wall Street's conventions, you'll never again have to fret over your portfolio. And once you get comfortable with this new approach, you might learn to ignore the research reports, best investment lists, economic news, and expert analysis that currently consume so much of your time and mental bandwidth. More free time and less worry—seems like an easy choice.

You may need to be reminded from time to time, though, that just because you're ignoring the financial news of the day doesn't mean you are mismanaging your investments. In fact, by lowering fees and minimizing the trading in a diversified portfolio, the average market return investor will come out ahead in the long run.

Just imagine if you could move most of your financial to-do list from the "urgent/important" box to the "not urgent/not important" box.

	URGENT	NOT URGENT
IMPORTANT	WORRY BUY / SELL STOCKS FOLLOW TV / NEWS EXPERTS SELECT INVESTMENT MANAGERS RESEARCH ECONOMIC DATA	
NOT IMPORTANT		

Step two of living in Wealthfulness is to stop following the outdated, expensive advice offered by Wall Street. The evidence clearly points to the benefits of a diversified market return portfolio. It's a simple, understandable approach to investing that has the answers to all of the questions we've discussed:

1. Why should you include stocks in your portfolio at all?
2. How should you invest?
3. What can you expect from markets?

3

Money and Your Brain: Making Better Financial Decisions

"Be fearful when others are greedy, and be greedy when others are fearful."

—*Warren Buffett[1]*

The previous chapter was meant to disrupt your conventional view of investing and begin a process of changing your paradigm when it comes to personal finance. When you adopt a market return philosophy, the planner in your head is free to focus on far more important aspects of your life and to do it with much less stress. But, as you'll soon see, that planner has a habit of making the same mistakes over and over again. Oh, and remember the elephant? You still have to deal with an emotional beast that can keep you from tackling all of the elements you need to address in your financial world.

In this chapter we'll talk about some of the connections between money and both sides of your brain—the logical and the emotional. All of your financial decisions are influenced by the values, experiences, and memories of your past. But can you trust them? You've got the investing part right; now you have to make yourself aware of the common behavioral pitfalls that can still sabotage your financial future—your Wealthfulness.

We naturally believe the rider in our head, the conscious part, is managing our day-to-day lives. We're making those lists, setting priorities, and checking things off throughout our day—we must be consciously managing it all, right? Not really. Our emotions have far greater influence over our decisions than we realize. Billions of calculations occur each day in our subconscious, each one subtly influencing our behavior before it rises to the level of conscious thought. There is simply no way you could drive a car, catch a football, or engage in a business meeting without your subconscious doing most of the work. Daniel Kahneman explains in his book *Thinking, Fast and Slow* that a lot of what goes on in our head as we make decisions is driven by memory and intuition.[2] Memory and intuition are part of the "fast" thinking Kahneman calls system 1, our elephant.

Driving from your home to the local grocery store primarily involves your system 1 in most cases. It doesn't require much of your mental attention, and you can easily chat, think, or sing to yourself while driving without any effort. Now imagine taking that same two-mile trip with your fifteen-year-old child or grandchild at the wheel. That kind of trip demands a much higher level of awareness, and so our slow thinking process, system 2, takes over.

All the decisions that happened automatically, subconsciously, turn into a series of logical commands—check your mirror; slow down; watch those kids on the bikes; turn right here, and then slowly get into the left lane. Wow, who knew how hard it was to drive a car? Bringing your subconsciously managed actions into awareness takes a lot of energy, which is why our brain is wired to take care of routine tasks with system 1. Our brains are coded to conserve our system 2 for slower, more intense mental processing.

Kahneman won a Nobel Prize in Economics for his research on how people make decisions using fast and slow thinking (system 1 and system 2), particularly how and why they repeatedly make mistakes in certain situations. His research explains how your thoughts are a nonstop string of connected ideas you can't usually describe. Stop reading this page for a second. Can you explain where the last three minutes of your thoughts came from? You may be able to recall the origins of a few strands if you're lucky. Those thoughts are running constantly in the back of your mind, connecting all your years of experience to the minute-to-minute events in your life.

Now think back to your first memory of money. Was it a good experience or bad? Has that memory influenced choices you made much later in life? Take a moment to let your mind wander. I've asked this simple question hundreds of times, and quite often people are surprised by the emotions that arise.

When I try this experiment myself, I go all the way back to the summer after fifth grade. I worked a paper route for a friend that summer while he was on vacation, and it earned me enough money to buy a used telescope. I spent the rest of that summer gazing at the craters and valleys of the moon in complete awe. I can also vividly re-member the payment book for my first car loan a few years later and how much I paid for those really expensive stereo speakers my parents hated. All of those sticky memories influence my personal picture of money.

Every one of us carries their own picture of money painted from their life experiences. However, we might not be as good at remembering our past as we believe. Kahneman and his good friend Amos Tversky spent much of their careers creating psychological experiments to show how our memories and intuitions are often wrong and can't be trusted.

So you have this emotional beast in your head, the elephant, that has a great deal of influence over your actions, and yet the research tells us that, quite unlike a real elephant, your memory can't be trusted. Your elephant forgets, misjudges, and is generally quite lazy. He or she is likely to default to what's easy or most pleasurable and couldn't care less about the future.

Your rider, on the other hand, is equally problematic. He or she will rely on shortcuts when faced with a complicated task; she tires easily and often hands over the reins to your emotions; and at times he's way too confident for his own good.

To avoid the poor decisions that can interfere with your long-term financial plan, you need to learn how to recognize the behavioral mistakes committed by both mental systems 1 (the elephant) and 2 (the rider).* We can sort these mistakes into three categories: emotional, rational, and universal.

Emotional mistakes come into play when our instincts and memory mislead us or allow our emotions to override our logical decision making process—this is when the elephant takes control. Our rational mistakes occur as we struggle to make sense of the world—i.e., the mental calculations and assumptions we constantly reference while making decisions. In this case, our rider is still in charge, but he's lost or confused. Finally, there are universal truths we can't avoid, no matter how hard our rider and elephant try to ignore them.

Avoiding Emotional Mistakes— Taming the Elephant

Black Monday—October 19, 1987

Over the last thirty years Kahneman, Tversky, and other researchers such as Richard Thaler and Robert Shiller have

---

* To summarize, the elephant (system 1) is designed to react quickly and effortlessly to routine decisions. The rider (system 2), on the other hand, is a slower, deeper thinking process requiring effort.

developed a new area of research in economics called behavioral economics. It is an area of study where economics, psychology, and neuroscience collaborate to understand the process of decision making. Along the way, these scientists have identified a long list of mistakes individuals make when they are confronted with choices. We tend to value the future far less than the present; we are generally very poor at understanding the effects of inflation or compounding returns; we remember our winning decisions much more than our losing ones; and we don't do well when it comes to understanding probabilities, large numbers, or statistics. All of which, by the way, are important elements when it comes to planning for your financial future.

One of the earliest findings in this area was the fact that people consistently ranked an experience of pain or pleasure by what is called the "peak-end rule." The pain level at the peak and then again at the end of an experience was a very good indicator of what would be reported by the participant. For example, test subjects would consistently prefer trials with much longer episodes of pain, and also higher average levels of pain, if the experiment had lower peaks or ended at a relatively low level of pain.[3]

When you think about it, this result is rather strange. Subjects will consistently prefer more total discomfort, as long as the pain at the end of the experiment is relatively low. We simply cannot evaluate unpleasant (or pleasant) experiences objectively—they are always subjectively related to our other recent experiences.

Lab studies using graduate students are interesting; however, we also have real-world examples from the global markets that show how this "peak-end rule" can influence investors' memories. I have met many people during my career who can vividly recall the market crash of 1987. To this day, their memories continue to influence their attitudes toward stock markets, and risk in general, thirty years after the experience.

Black Monday, as the day became known, occurred on October 19, 1987, and at the time I was living in the Grammercy Park area of Manhattan. My parents were visiting from Texas, and we just happened to be watching from the visitors' box on the New York Stock Exchange when the final bell rang at 4 p.m. on Black Monday. As we walked home to my apartment that afternoon I was sure we had witnessed the beginning of the next Great Depression. The Dow Industrial index fell over 22 percent on Black Monday, and the broader S&P 500 index fell over 20 percent.

Now let's look at the returns for the S&P 500 during the years before and after October 19, 1987:

1985	31.25%
1986	18.49%
1987	**5.81%**
1988	16.54%
1989	31.48%

Does that five-year period look like it could leave an indelible impression on investors thirty years later? Does the year 1987 look that bad to you?

Why are so many people haunted by their memory of that year? People remember that loss because at its peak the market pain was a 20 percent drop in one day. Regardless of how 1987 fared from January to September, that painful memory stays with them. The trouble is this kind of "sticky" memory can influence your saving and spending behavior many decades later, sabotaging your best efforts to follow a long-term financial plan. Painful losses create emotional baggage that can lead to financial mistakes much later in life.

The tech bust in the early 2000s and the financial crisis in 2008 had similar effects on millions of investors. I believe our younger generations will be less prepared financially because of the stress they witnessed their parents go through in 2000 and 2008. They have less faith in capitalism and in markets.

Remember, Wealthfulness is simply a thoughtful process for expressing your goals and then setting a course to achieve those goals. Maybe it's a first house or a college education for your kids, possibly a lake cabin or more disposable income, but whatever your goals may be, not much will happen without a plan for saving and investing in markets. The funny thing is, when you examine most of your goals, they are usually tied to fundamental emotional needs like peace of mind, security, and happiness. You simply cannot break the bond between money and emotions; those past money memories are there to stay, and they may be undermining your faith in markets.

> Question: Are your distant financial memories clouding your judgment and obscuring the financial course you've set? Do you and your spouse share similar feelings about money?

The Trust Paradox—Do You Still Trust Your Bank?

For decades investors have been led to believe that financial markets are scary. Markets are risky, they are told, so consumers are naturally inclined to trust the big banks with brand names they recognize. Let's be very clear—markets are not scary, they're simply volatile from day to day. Big banks are scary.

Think for a moment about the most important transactions and the most trusted service providers in your life—your doctor and dentist, your child's daycare, your financial advisor, realtor, or insurance broker. If you are like most people, you chose almost all of these providers based exclusively on a friend or family recommendation.

Whether it's your child's care, your health, your retirement, or the largest purchase you'll ever make—a home—trust is paramount. It's essential.

Ronald J. Baker, in his book *Implementing Value Pricing*, tells us these types of services, called credence products, "have attributes buyers cannot confidently evaluate, even after one or more purchases."[4] Because a buyer cannot see, touch, or easily measure something like advice, they are more reliant on brand names. Customers also place more emphasis on testimonials and recommendations from people they know.

There are very few industries that require as much trust as banking and finance. You give the banks and brokerage firms your money, and you trust they will return it to you some day in the future. In the meantime, you must trust that your money is somewhere safe and secure and that the statements you're receiving reflect the real value of your investment. Sadly, there will always be people like Bernie Madoff breaking that trust. You could be handing over your entire life savings or a college fund for your kids, and yet you have nothing tangible to hold onto in exchange for your money.

Wall Street banks know they must be trusted—their existence depends on it. But for years we've witnessed scandal after scandal in the financial industry. They have manipulated interest rates, rigged the municipal bond market, cheated mutual fund investors, and put the entire world economy at risk during the financial crisis of 2008. Global banks have paid more than $300 billion in fines between 2008 and 2016, and we're still counting.[5] So how, in spite of decades of scandals, have these "too big to fail" monstrosities managed to survive?

And survive they have. JPMorgan, the nation's second-largest bank by assets, has more than fifty million customers.[6] Merrill Lynch, now a part of Bank of America, manages more than $2.4 trillion for their investment clients.[7] Clearly, these financial behemoths have Americans' money, but why on earth do they have their trust?

As explained on the Financial Trust website when the index was introduced in 2009,

. . . economic models cannot explain the deep recession we are quickly sliding into. There was no apparent shock to productivity nor a clear slowdown in innovation. The government has kept taxes low. The Federal Reserve has kept interest rates low and cut them even further. Yet, everyone agrees that this crisis originated in the financial system.

Why? Because something important was destroyed in the last few months. It is an asset crucial to production, even if it is not made of bricks and mortar. This asset is TRUST.[9]

This question is so crucial, and so puzzling, two professors of finance created something called the Quarterly Financial Trust Index in order to measure our trust in these institutions.[8] Banks have generally fared better than mutual funds or large corporations in the survey, and there is almost universal mistrust for the stock market, with numbers as low as 12 percent in early 2011.

The year following the Great Recession, in December of 2009, the survey found only about one-third (35 percent) of those polled trusted national banks; this was

71

lower than the trust in credit unions (56 percent) and local banks (59 percent).

Six years later, in December of 2015, the number of those surveyed who trusted the national banks still hovered close to 30 percent.

One of the creators of the index, Professor Luigi Singales, told me the numbers get even worse if you look at only the "too-big-to-fail" national banks bailed out by the government. For them, the trust level is bouncing along the bottom somewhere between 20 and 25 percent.

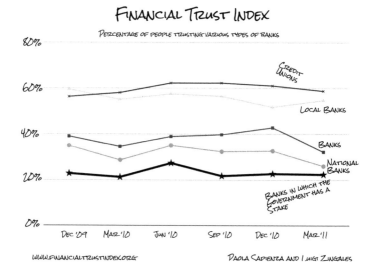

FINANCIAL TRUST INDEX

PERCENTAGE OF PEOPLE TRUSTING VARIOUS TYPES OF BANKS

WWW.FINANCIALTRUSTINDEX.ORG   PAOLA SAPIENZA AND LUIGI ZINGALES

Think about that. Only one in four Americans trust the nation's largest banks, and yet these institutions invest trillions of dollars for the very same people.

Consumers flock to the big banks because they recognize those brands after many, many years of brilliant marketing. For decades, the financial services industry has been one of the largest advertising and lobbying groups in the country, spending close to $100 million each year on lobbying and almost $7 billion on branding through digital media in 2015 alone.[10]

Generations of Americans have watched television commercials where some fading celebrity with no knowledge of finance promotes a well-known financial conglomerate. Or perhaps they have watched one of the ads with a fictitious advisor and his client as they attend a child's wedding or walk the beach together in retirement.

These ads work because they affect your emotional attachment and trust in the brand by way of something psychologists call the affect heuristic. Professor Kahneman describes this as a process where people make decisions based on their feeling about something or someone—their emotions—rather than logic or reasoning.

A heuristic is simply a shortcut for making decisions, and we use them constantly every day. We couldn't survive without our shortcuts, because the world is far too complex to analyze every decision and every situation. These shortcuts allow us to conserve our mental bandwidth while still being able to quickly process the hundreds of interactions we experience daily.

Just imagine for a moment going through your day and stopping at each interaction to give it your complete attention. Most people would be exhausted shortly after they left Starbucks and made their way into the office. Is the interaction safe, fair, reasonable, valuable? Does the math make sense? Is it worth my time? Could I find a better option? Will the situation change? Heuristic shortcuts allow our elephant to make decisions subconsciously in milliseconds without engaging the conscious rider who (as usual) thinks he's in control.

But heuristics also lead us into emotional decisions that exclude our rational side. Whether it's buying a car or choosing a bank, an emotionally based decision might not result in the best outcomes. The big banks and insurance companies are exceptionally good at appealing to our emotions and short-circuiting the logical side of our brains.

Maybe it's time to rethink some of those trusted relationships you've had for years—does that credit card company you've been with for decades or that insurance company your father recommended when you were seventeen really have your best interests in mind? Loyalty is one of the most fundamental human characteristics; however, it can be manipulated or go unreciprocated. Your natural instincts may have led you into many emotional decisions that are not in your best interests.

False Assumptions Can Distort Our View of the World

Composition Fallacy

Try this mental exercise. Imagine that we want to spend whatever it takes to build the best car money can buy. First I ask you to go out and get the most advanced engine in the world. Then I send you out again for the best suspension currently being produced. We work our way sequentially through the list of parts, scouring the world for the greatest transmissions, electronics, wheels, cooling system, etc.

Once we have everything collected in one large facility, we bring in the best German, Japanese, and American engineers we can find. We put all our resources at their disposal and set them to work. An hour later, the lead engineer comes to us with a disheartening report. None of the best parts in the world were designed to work together—the car is going to be a disaster.

You and I have just fallen into the Composition Fallacy. The very best pieces of something may not come together as a great whole. This happens in sports, business, blockbuster movies, and many other examples. It's a fact of life.

Most families approach their financial planning in much the same way we tried to build that car. They tackle one issue at a time, assuming their best effort on the current problem at hand will work just fine with everything already in place. We see it all the time—after weeks of research and worry, a client will call to explain his thoughtful solution for an immediate financial concern. Unfortunately, the solution he's found would completely undermine another part of the financial plan he didn't consider.

By far, the most common mistake we see is the single-minded rush to avoid taxes at all costs. As the old saying goes, "don't let the tax tail wag the dog." Traditional IRAs and 401(k)s are good examples. These tax deferral tools are often overused or misunderstood. As a result, many people wind up in retirement with almost all their savings in IRA or 401(k) accounts, which makes tax planning during retirement much more difficult.

Take a look at your investment balances—do you have most of your savings in a tax-deferred account like a SEP, 401(k), or IRA? Those accounts may be great for reducing your taxes while you're working, but you'll eventually be forced to withdraw money and pay taxes when you reach age seventy and a half. Unfortunately, if you have a $100,000 IRA account, you don't own one hundred thousand dollars. The government will likely take about 25 percent of your money in taxes, so your piece is closer to $75,000.

A better plan would be to consider your current tax burden *and* your future annual tax projections. Oftentimes, it makes sense to a pay a bit more in taxes in some years to help reduce your taxes in other years. But you need a long-term plan to make the analysis possible. Ideally, you should strive to enter retirement with three buckets of money—tax-free Roth accounts; tax-deferred IRAs or 401(k)s; and after-tax investment/savings accounts. These differently taxed buckets give you more flexibility to control your taxes when you're spending down the accounts during retirement.

The goal is to pay the least amount of legitimate taxes possible over your lifetime, not get your taxes as low as possible each year. They are absolutely not the same thing.

Another example is how families typically approach the benefits offered through their employer. Quite often spouses sign up each year for benefits from their individual companies without coordinating their options. Sure, it takes some work to coordinate your options, but the risks and rewards are worth considering. Do you both—independently—have enough coverage for your life and disability? Are you both taking the full advantage of your employer retirement account and health-care options? What would happen if either spouse lost their job—what benefits could not be replaced easily?

A financial plan is like a giant suspended mobile—every time you move one piece, other pieces will move automatically as the system changes. Successful financial planning is not about the individual pieces; it's about the whole picture.

Overconfidence—Are You Too Confident in Your Investing Skills and Your Future?

Humans are naturally optimistic, a trait that has served us well over the last ten thousand years. Overconfidence helps us take important societal risks, like having children, for instance. Admit it, parents—far fewer people would have a child if they fully understood the amount of time, financial resources, and energy it required.

I would do it again in a minute, but I must admit I was just lucky. We weren't financially prepared at all for our first child—I had just started a new career, my wife was working in an entry-level retail job, and we didn't have wills or nearly enough life insurance.

So it is with lots of the choices we make in life. Entrepreneurs like Steve Jobs start companies in their garages; small business owners hire new employees anticipating new customers; counties build roads well in advance of the population growth—all of these choices require optimism, and we're all better off for it.

Unfortunately, optimism also has a dark side—too much risk taking. Economists Terence Odean and Brad Barber have shown in their studies of brokerage accounts that overconfidence is directly linked to excessive trading.[11] Excessive traders, not surprisingly, turn out to be terrible investors, and they are overwhelmingly male. Sorry, men, but the research suggests women are better investors, because they trade less and show more patience with their trades.

Overconfidence may have implications for the global economy as well. Researchers in psychology, economics, and various other fields are now finding evidence connecting the male-dominated, aggressive environment typical of Wall Street to the excessive risk taking and poor decisions that led to the Great Recession of 2008.[12]

Optimism can lead to a host of problems when it comes to a family's financial plan, too. With that extra dose of confidence, it's easier to avoid saving for retirement or college. And excess optimism can lead to underinsurance for the real risks your family faces, like disability or death of the main breadwinner.

Who Takes the Risk, and Who Bears the Cost?

Several years ago I met with a nice couple in their late fifties. Their kids were out of the house, the credit cards were paid off, and they were ready to get serious about financial planning. What they weren't ready for was reality.

The husband proclaimed early in our meeting that he was a big risk taker and proud of it. "I've taken big risks my whole life, and I'm comfortable with that," he said. Their portfolio, sure enough, had plenty of risky investments to prove his point. Unfortunately, the list of other risks he was taking but not willing to acknowledge was quite long.

For starters, this couple had not saved nearly enough for retirement, and their lifestyle didn't suggest there was much room for additional savings. The husband had no life insurance or disability insurance, even though he was the major breadwinner. To make matters worse, he needed to work until at least age seventy to meet their retirement goals, despite having medical issues and a family history on both sides of dying young.

Yes, he was a huge risk taker, but the real question was—who benefited and who suffered the consequences of those risks?

I have seen firsthand what can happen to a family when the main breadwinner dies. I never knew either one of my grandfathers, who both died before I was born. No one ever talked about it while I was growing up, but I witnessed the kind of lives that were left for my widowed grandmothers, who were both still raising young children. Those kinds of events change the course of life for everyone in the family for generations. Dreams die, choices fade away, and what remains is a lot of hard work and what-ifs for the people left behind. Grief turns out to be surprisingly expensive in time, energy, and money, and it's the children and future generations who suffer most.

Choosing to have little or no insurance for health, disability, and death will definitely save your family money in the short run. You are guaranteed to have more discretionary income to spend as long as you are healthy and alive. Who is the biggest winner if everything turns out okay? Obviously, it's the main breadwinner, who has more money to spend while still healthy. Who loses if things don't turn out so rosy? The family left behind.

The problem is that, in the present, the breadwinner and the family enjoy an immediate benefit of more money; but who is considering the long-term risks? The situation is complicated because the social default for most families is to have the husband take care of financial issues, even when the wife is more qualified. We are all naturally over-optimistic about our own life expectancy, and who wants to talk about dying? Unfortunately, the kids don't usually have a say in this important aspect of their future.

It's more likely the dependent spouse does have a say in a decision regarding insurance; however, they face four significant challenges if they are going to take care of their family:

1. Admitting the realistic possibility of a bad outcome where the main breadwinner dies.
2. Calculating their insurance need, which can be challenging for most people.
3. Making the tough choice to reduce their current spending to buy insurance and protect against this risk.
4. Convincing the optimistic spouse to agree to reduce their spending, too.

Let's say you're a forty-five-year-old male with a spouse and young family. Purchasing insurance to protect your family from the risk of your disability or death could cost several thousand dollars per year. How do you assess that risk?

Miscalculations and Misestimations—Why We're Not Very Good at Financial Planning

Researchers have been studying how people assess risk for decades, and they've concluded humans are not very good at mental math in these kinds of situations. Again, we tend to use a natural shortcut, called the availability heuristic, to help us quickly solve many risk-estimation problems. Our ancestors didn't have the time or mental computing power to statistically analyze the situations they encountered—the ones who stopped to think about a problem got eaten. Instead, our ancestors used their recent memory to make a quick guess using the data immediately available to them.

Our forty-five-year-old father will typically resort to the availability shortcut to assess his need for insurance. If he has had a friend or family member who died young, his assessment may overstate the risk he faces. The reverse, however, is more often the case. It's likely this father can't think of a single person his age who died or was disabled, and so he proceeds to underestimate his risk.

Take this father's natural wiring for overconfidence, add a quick (mis)estimate of the risk, and you get another family exposed to far too much risk unnecessarily. Sure, the chance that a male will die in his forty-fifth year is less than 1 percent, but is that really the question you should be asking? Because the risk of an underinsured widow and her family suffering hardship, stress, and regret is close to 100 percent.

Just like in the last chapter on investing, you may be in need of a new, more effective paradigm when it comes to risk. I can't begin to tell you how many clients I've talked to who said they hate insurance. Seriously, folks, the insurance process is doomed to fail if you're looking for a pleasant experience. Life is risky; you will inevitably suffer a cost, a loss, or both.

Many years ago, I had the pleasure of interviewing Peter Bernstein, author of the book *Against the Gods: The Remarkable Story of Risk*. It was, unquestionably, one of my favorite interviews. His wife, Barbara, answered the phone when we called and said they had just finished lunch. We chatted with Barbara for awhile, talking about their weather in New York and ours in Dallas as Peter prepared for our interview. I could just imagine them in a cozy, book-filled flat, many stories above a bustling New York street.

Bernstein was well into his eighties by then, but the minute he picked up the phone it felt like your favorite professor had just started a lecture on your favorite topic. So many stories and so many insights to cover in such a short time.

Against the Gods is a wonderfully engaging story of how humans discovered the concept of risk and eventually learned to manage it using inventions like insurance. As Bernstein argues in the book, it was the eventual understanding of risk that allowed early societies to step out of their self-limiting world. We had to understand the nature of probability before we could take calculated risks that improved the world and advanced our societies. All of the world's past empires were built on calculated risks.

As Bernstein writes in his introduction, "Without insurance in its many varieties, the death of the breadwinner would reduce young families to starvation or charity, even more people would be denied health care, and only the wealthiest could afford to own a home."[13]

Insurance payments are intended to be a waste of money for most of the people paying them—whether it's for your health, your property, or your life. If that weren't the case, there wouldn't be enough money left to pay the claims for the unlucky few who needed it. This is a fantastic way for society to insure against the catastrophic risks we all hope to avoid individually during our lifetime.

Unfortunately, far too many consumers misunderstand the purpose of real insurance, which is to protect you against the catastrophic loss, not the everyday accident or mishap that we all experience from time to time. In the end, those insurance premiums will turn out to be a very lucky waste of cash or the best money you ever spent. That may require a paradigm shift for many people.

> Question: Are you certain you've protected the most valuable things and people in your life? Is your assessment of risk reasonable and responsible? How will your family fare if things turn out bad? Would your spouse and children agree with your choices?

Discounting the Future

A financial plan is in many ways just a negotiation between the you of today and a future you. One of the two will get to enjoy the resources you accumulate over your lifetime, and a financial plan helps you make that decision purposefully. Saving more in the present will give the future you more money to spend. And, conversely, choosing to save less, or none at all, in the present is shortchanging that future self. This tradeoff becomes much more complicated when more than one person is involved—spouses, kids, and grandkids are all vying for their share now and in the future.

Early economists assumed people were fairly consistent and logical when it came to making decisions about the future. However, over the last thirty years, they've come to realize this isn't typically how it works. We all tend to discount the future, oftentimes in inconsistent or illogical ways. For example, in one study participants were asked to state how much money it would take for them to trade $15 today for some amount at a future date; either one month, one year, or ten years. The researchers concluded that the average person would require $20 one month in the future to make them indifferent to receiving $15 immediately. That turns out to be an annualized rate of return of more than 300 percent. The same tradeoff required a rate of return of 120 percent over twelve months ($50) and a substantially lower rate of only 19 percent over ten years ($100).[14]

You might be asking at this point what these conclusions have to do with you and your financial world. You generally don't get approached with this type of problem. Or do you? Is it possible the financial and marketing industries are aware of these preferences and subtly use them against you? The unavoidable truth is there will always be a connection between cost and benefit—you won't find much for free in life. With sophisticated marketing tools and an understanding of your behavioral mistakes, companies can obscure that connection between what you want and how much you will eventually pay for it.

How much is all of that immediate gratification costing you?

Let's look at an easy example. Do you find yourself spending more on something to get it sooner? Spending $5 for shipping on a $50 item will cost you 10 percent, or a little over 3 percent each day if it arrives three days earlier. But if you annualized that $5 over the three days it saved you, your convenience cost turns into an annualized interest rate of over 1000 percent. If you are making this kind of convenience decision daily, you may be shocked at how much your discounting of the future is costing you.

Deciding to buy that Starbucks Venti or save for college has the same profile. The enjoyment is here today, while that looming cost of college is far off in the future. If we displayed both costs in today's dollars, right there on the Starbucks menu, it would take your breath away as you walked out empty handed.

For most people, future costs or benefits are very difficult to estimate relative to today's costs or benefits, whether it's the well-trained waiter sabotaging your diet with a dessert suggestion, the car dealership offering a seven-year loan, or the financial services industry and most of their products. Your natural discounting of the future puts you at a distinct disadvantage when marketers are trying to sell you something.

Loss Aversion—We Really, Really Hate to Lose Money

At this point you might be worried your discounting of the future puts you at a disadvantage, but it's nothing compared to your aversion to losses.

Professor Kahneman offers a simple question to help estimate your own loss aversion: How much of a gain would it take to make you indifferent between that gain and a loss of $100 if the chances were equal?[15] Would you bet $100 on a coin toss if you could win $120? How about $150—no? In his studies, Kahneman found that most people settle around $200 (200 percent), while other studies put the loss aversion percentage somewhere between 150 and 250 percent. This is far more than classical economists would have predicted with their theories based on rational human actors.

Your distaste for losing turns out to be a goldmine for the financial industry. While you're inclined to pay far more than necessary to avoid losses, the industry is always happy to offer products that can address those fears—for a hefty price.

Variable annuities are a good example. Annual sales for these notoriously complicated products have exceeded $130 billion over the last decade. Their popularity is due, in large part, to their promise not to lose your money. Yes, there are guarantees included in most annuities that protect your initial investment, but those guarantees typically come at a very high cost. Investors often end up paying more than 3 percent each year for the "benefit" of not losing money.

Variable annuities are financial products custom-designed to exploit your natural loss aversion. Not surprisingly, sales for these products typically skyrocket after a market downturn, exactly when investors should be thinking about future market returns and not past losses, i.e., the worst possible time to consider an annuity.

When you look at the academic literature on annuities or visit the US Securities and Exchange Commission website (at SEC.gov), you'll find lots of warnings when it comes to these products and their expensive promises.[16] Virtually every financial journalist has been warning about these products for decades, yet they continue to be exceptionally popular with unsophisticated investors who are motivated by loss aversion.

Be very, very careful—annuities are complicated, expensive, and designed by an industry that does not have your interests in mind.**

Obviously, saving the 3 percent annual fee you're paying for an annuity would get investors a long way toward their goal. When you do the math and read the annuity contracts, you'll usually find there are far simpler and less expensive ways to achieve the same goals. Investors, however, don't do the math or read the contracts. In fact, if you're reading this book right now and you own an annuity, I can say with confidence it is highly unlikely you've read the contract your broker gave you. Even worse, you have no idea how much you're paying in fees for your "safety."

Loss aversion can also lead retirees to rely too heavily on bonds once they stop working. The conventional argument has always been stocks are too risky for retirees once they no longer have a salary to rely on, so they should

---

** There are several types of annuities—indexed, variable, and immediate. Immediate annuities deserve a separate discussion and, when used properly, can be excellent, low-cost tools for building a retirement plan. Don't confuse immediate annuities with the less appealing other types of annuities—variable and indexed.

stick to bonds and live off of the interest. As we've already discussed in chapter 2, that kind of outdated thinking has failed investors just as badly as Wall Street banks and brokerage firms. We live in a world where thirty-year US Treasury bonds are paying around 3 percent, making it impossible for most retirees to live off only the interest.

Retirees need a healthy dose of stocks in their portfolio if they are going to maintain their lifestyle over a thirty-year retirement, along with a comprehensive financial plan to help them understand their cash flow over such a long period. Previous generations didn't have this problem. They weren't planning for three decades in retirement. Remember, a $50,000 lifestyle at sixty years old turns into a $100,000 lifestyle by the time you're eighty-four, if you want to keep up with 3 percent inflation.[***]

Stocks are one of the only ways to keep up with inflation, but you cannot avoid losses in the market from time to time. That's where the financial plan comes in. You will be much more prepared for market drops, financially and mentally, if you have already considered your income,

---

[***] Using the Rule of 72—your cost will double in 7.2 years at 10 percent (72/10). With 3 percent inflation your costs will double in twenty-four years (72/3).

spending, and portfolio growth over your next thirty years. You can make conservative assumptions and adjustments from year to year—if you have a plan to work from.

The Arrow of Time—You Can't Change the Past

As we close out this chapter, let me leave you with one final concept that relates to your future financial plans and the challenges you face in achieving your goals. Regardless of how well you've planned for your future, all things decay over time. We lose our health, earning potential, and time on earth as we age. None of us like to think of life this way; nevertheless, this truth is fundamental to our financial well-being.

We simply don't have the same options for life insurance coverage after a heart attack or bout with cancer. We can't save more of our income once we've retired or take back all of those hard-earned dollars we thoughtlessly wasted before we had kids. The bottom line is we cannot change the past.

You should understand by now how the emotional side of your brain works to sabotage your goals. That elephant doesn't want to talk about dying or save for a future far off in the distance. But your procrastination can have irreversible consequences that are almost always negative.

In chapter 5 we'll talk about some tools from behavioral finance that might move your elephant along in the right direction.

Your emotional connection to money, your trust in the financial system, and your behavioral biases all influence the decisions you make and, ultimately, the security and peace of mind you're able to attain for yourself and your family. In this chapter, I've shown you just a small sample of the psychological biases that may be impeding your financial success. You cannot simply pick up the phone and call some expert to solve these issues right away. You must accept the idea that money is tied to your emotions and your memories. Understand that you and/or your spouse may be overconfident when it comes to finances and that serious risks to your lifestyle and retirement are possibly being ignored.

A Wealthfulness mind-set will weave purpose into your financial decisions, shifting your attention away from the distractions of today and allowing you to focus your energy on the future.

Step three of living in Wealthfulness is to recognize and understand your behavioral biases and how they can interfere with your financial goals.

NOW we're ready to talk about what that future looks like.

4

Money and Happiness: Rethinking the Relationship

"Money has never made man happy,
nor will it; there is nothing in its
nature to produce happiness."

—*Benjamin Franklin[1]*

Can money buy happiness? It's a question philosophers have asked for millennia. While there is still plenty of debate on the topic in economics, just about everyone agrees money can only get you so far when it comes to happiness. That is, a lot more money only makes you a little bit happier, if at all.

As Ben Casnocha, an entrepreneur and best-selling author based in Silicon Valley, noted when it comes to billionaires, "Some of them are quite happy . . . But many of them are not happy or have prolonged bouts of unhappiness—even though they're way ahead in the global rat race."[2]

If billions of dollars might not be enough, what can we conclude about money and happiness? Well, one recent study has even given us a number to work with—$75,000.[3] According to Angus Deaton and Daniel Kahneman, both Nobel Laureates in Economics, an annual family income of $75,000 could take you to the top level of emotional happiness. Anything more than that might get you more things to buy and more social status, but it probably won't add much to your long-term happiness.

Stop for a moment and ask yourself how you feel about that number. Would $75,000 be enough for you? If not, then why? How much would be enough?

Despite the evidence, the financial services industry continues to ignore the fact that money and happiness are only distant cousins. They prefer instead to pretend the two are close, intimate friends. This is because the bank and brokerage business model is built on a single promise—more money. Wall Street sells greed because that's something you can put a number on. If you want to double your money, reach $1 million or retire by the time you're fifty, Wall Street has a plan to sell you. But Wall Street only knows how to keep score in dollars.

Happiness, well, that's not so easy to put a number on. It can't be hedged or shorted, and you can't put it in a presentation with flashy charts and graphs. If you're interested in something more than money—if you're looking for happiness or a meaningful life—Wall Street can't help you.

It's up to you to envision a future that
includes a lot more than just money.

Happiness is clearly an important concept, or so the Founding Fathers thought. They imbued our Declaration of Independence with its importance, holding happiness out as a standard for the citizenry:

We hold these truths to be self-evident, that all men
are created equal, that they are endowed by their
Creator with certain unalienable Rights, that among
these are Life, Liberty and the pursuit of Happiness.

Research tells us factors such as good health, friends, freedom, security, and trust are all important to our long-term happiness. Conversely, factors like unemployment, inflation, and chronic pain chip away at the joy we find in life.

Maybe money cannot buy you happiness, but what if there were a formula that could point the way to a deeper and wider range of happiness in your life? Enter happiness research—a confluence of research from the fields of neuroscience, sociology, psychology, and economics—which is shedding new light on what truly makes us happy. And, unlike most current work in economics, the research on happiness provides answers we can immediately apply to our everyday lives.

The formula for happiness turns out to be fairly straightforward: H = S + C +V.[4]

> **H** = sustained happiness. Not the kind you get from a piece of chocolate cake or a great first date but rather the kind of ongoing happiness you carry with you throughout your life. The type of real happiness humans long for and our Founding Fathers had in mind.

> **S** = your individual set point. This is your natural level of happiness, akin to your body temperature or heart rate. They may go up or down for periods of time, but your temperature and heart rate will eventually settle back to your natural, steady state.

Your level of happiness behaves the same way. In fact, researchers have found that even multimillion-dollar lottery winners eventually settle back into their previous level of happiness. There is a wide range to set-point happiness, and some people are naturally happier than others. This doesn't mean you are powerless when it comes to your happiness, however. The good news is less than 50 percent of your happiness is attributable to your set point, which means you can control much of your own happiness if you choose to.

C = conditions in your life. These are the things you cannot change in your life, such as your race, age, or childhood family situation, and things that may change slowly over some extended period of time, like marital status and occupation. Think of conditions as the elements of your life that remain relatively constant from one day to the next. The good news here is humans are very, very adaptable to the conditions in their lives. Even serious cancer patients and impoverished third-world communities can report relatively high degrees of happiness.

And finally,

V = voluntary activities which you have immediate control over. Prayer, meditation, social involvement, exercise, and volunteering are all examples of the kinds of choices you can make regarding your time, money, and energy from day to day and hour to hour that can have a lasting impact on your happiness.

In short, there are lots of things that can affect your happiness—some you can change and some you can't. This chapter is about taking the emphasis off money—something that will probably have very little influence on your happiness—and focusing on the voluntary activities that just might make you happy for the rest of your life.

Your conditions do not define your
happiness, unless you let them.

Choice Conflict—Limit Your Options If You Want to Be Happier

Like many of the concepts we'll discuss regarding happiness, too much of a good thing can lead to less happiness. Take choices for example; we know from the research that greater control over your living space, career path, and representative government—just to name a few examples—can significantly improve your happiness.[5] Humans want to have choices when it comes to their environment. However, too many choices can paralyze you, often leading to no choice being made at all. Professor Barry Schwarz describes this as the paradox of choice.[6]

Choice overload, as he calls it, encroaches into our everyday lives in powerful ways—from our trips to the grocery store to the investments we make in our 401(k)s. In the early 90s I studied Russian from an amazing professor in Washington, DC. He was a native Russian speaker but also fluent in English, French, Greek, and probably a few other languages I wasn't aware of. In addition to his teaching workload, my professor volunteered his time helping Soviet emigrants assimilate into their new lives in the United States. Remember, these were the first few years of "Perestroika," Russia was still part of the Soviet Union, and hundreds of thousands of Russians were fleeing to the West each year.

Those Russians had rarely experienced freedom of choice in more than four generations. Choosing a career or where to live were not unbounded options for most Soviet citizens. My professor would take these new arrivals shopping and help them search for jobs and find housing in the Washington, DC, area. The stories he retold to our evening class were tragic, real-life examples of choice overload.

Even the simple process of choosing toothpaste or cereal for their kids could be overwhelming in the West. Where they were used to one or two options on the shelves in Moscow, they now faced one or two aisles of choices, four rows high. Incredibly, my professor shared more than one story of families returning to Russia because they were simply unprepared for the massive range of choices their new lives offered.

In his book *The Paradox of Choice*, Barry Schwartz challenges the idea that having more choices is always better for us. In fact, he argues that seeking the very best may actually leave us worse off. By setting your standard to "the best," you may be condemning yourself to a relentless feeling of "what if." What if I had acted sooner; waited longer; done more research; known about this or that resource? Schwartz calls this "maximizing," and this type of behavior can be counterproductive.

In effect, Schwartz recommends we lower our standards. Striving for "good enough" will lead to happier and healthier lives, with less stress and far more time for the important people who matter. He calls it "satisficing," and it may be the solution in our age of too much information and too many choices. But you must choose to strive for "good enough." It might not feel natural, may even seem like losing to some, because as a culture we tend to place a high value on winning. Will "good enough" be good enough to feel as if it was a success?

This is where Wealthfulness comes into play. You have a choice—to win the battle or win the war. Wealthfulness is a mind-set that can lead to a healthy, happy, and full life, but it might just entail satisficing when your natural inclination is to maximize. "The Best" is just today's little skirmish—occasionally important, but probably not.

Running Toward a Number

"The elephant cares about prestige, not happiness."[7]

One of the most interesting findings in the happiness research is the universal tendency for humans to prefer relative wealth over absolute wealth. What this means is a wealthy farmer in China with a few cows will generally report feeling just as happy as a wealthy farmer in Texas with a herd of six hundred cows. People tend to compare themselves with other people in their community, and consequently their happiness can rise or fall depending on where they see themselves in comparison to those around them. This might be why you often see a highly successful sibling or in-law as the antagonist in movies and books; they become constant reminders of our relative wealth.

I would venture to say the most frequent question I'm asked when discussing someone's financial plan is, "How are we doing compared to everyone else?" The correct answer is, of course, it doesn't matter.

Lee Eisenberg wrote a book several years back called *The Number*, in which he argued everyone has a "number"—the money in the bank they want to have when they retire. Eisenberg got the idea for his book from his conversations with Wall Street bankers and traders, who he said ALWAYS had a number.[8]

The interesting thing, though, is Eisenberg found the number would change as their salaries and bonuses inflated. Their number got bigger because everyone around them was receiving a lot more money, too. Who could be happy with $2 million in retirement, which seemed like so much money at one point, if it's less than your friend's bonus last year?

It's not the amount of wealth, but what
you have relative to your neighbors.

This idea of comparing ourselves to those around us and constantly trying to keep up is related to something psychologists call the hedonic treadmill. The idea is derived from the word hedonism, meaning the pursuit of pleasure. The hedonic treadmill is simply a constant and increasing cycle of materialism in search of pleasure.

As Carol Graham points out in her book *The Pursuit of Happiness*, "increasing levels of income—and income growth—tend to be accompanied by rising expectations and related frustrations."[9] Having more can make you want even more, which can lead to increasing stress and frustration and eventually to a lower level of happiness.

One of my most enduring memories as a financial planner is of an elderly gentleman with considerable wealth—more than his family could spend over several generations. Having grown up during years of unrest in Colombia, he was terrified of losing even a little bit of his money. One day I had the pleasure of hearing him reminisce about his life when he was young and in love. He and his future wife, owning virtually nothing but a beat-up motorcycle, would ride through the streets of Bogota in the summer evenings. You could almost feel the wind as he told his story, his bride of fifty years smiling beside him.

He looked up at me and sighed, "We were happier then."

A Wealthfulness mind-set helps you step off that treadmill by forcing you to communicate your financial priorities and reassess your definition of success. My client was realizing in his eighth decade of life that it wasn't the money or his success as an architect that mattered most. It was his life experiences with his wife, his family, and the memories of his youth in Colombia that resonated. All the money, in fact, was making him quite unhappy.

In the end, experiences create much deeper memories than material things. Friends and travel, for example, build longer-lasting memories than the new car that slowly becomes just a car. This is true partly because our memories are far more malleable than we think—remember from the last chapter how our emotions, the elephant, could influence our recollection of an experience? Researchers have suggested that it is far easier to mold an experience than it is a material object. The experience is more subjective, more open to interpretation.

As Eisenberg wisely points out in his book, experiences are almost always less expensive and easier to come by than precious material things. He suggests, in the end, that the unexamined life is much more expensive, because those mindless material purchases never truly fill the empty void in our lives.

Conspicuous Consumption—Who's Watching What You Buy?

If the research is correct in telling us that experiences matter more than material things, why are Americans still racing along on their hedonic treadmills—reaching for bigger houses, driving more expensive cars, and following the Kardashians on social media instead of hiking the Rockies with their kids?

Robert Frank, an economist at Cornell University, has spent decades trying to understand why people often behave in such irrational ways. Like many of the economists we've discussed so far, Frank has concluded that we are not the purely rational, self-interested creatures depicted in Adam Smith's *Wealth of Nations*. Frank points out, for example, that we like others to see what we are consuming—i.e., we want our neighbors and friends to see where our money goes. He calls this conspicuous consumption, and it has a surprisingly large role in how we make purchasing decisions. The houses we buy, the cars we drive, and the clothes we wear are all, to some degree, bought with others in mind.

Frank's insight is that a bigger home or a new car is conspicuous, while a longer vacation or quality time with your family is not.[10] Your neighbors and friends may not even notice the quality time you spend with your kids, but they're sure to notice that new BMW. Consequently, we subconsciously (or even consciously) opt for the material objects that give us only temporary happiness, rather than the experiences that enrich our lives and make them more memorable. Wouldn't we all be better off with longer vacations and shorter commutes, rather than suffering the incessant trend toward suburban McMansions and 24/7 job stress?

Think for a moment about your most recent purchases. Have there been more material items or experiences? How conspicuous? Do you rely on brands, labels, and high prices to lend credibility to what you buy?

Interestingly, our digitally connected lives may be leading to positive changes in our conspicuous consumption. Economist Tyler Cowen points out that people are obviously emphasizing experiences, i.e., leisure, as they flock to social media to document their evenings, food, and travel.[11] Nowadays they can instantly share those great pictures of Italy or Cancun with hundreds of Facebook friends. So maybe, just maybe, Facebook is encouraging us to connect with more people in meaningful ways—to share experiences instead of things. Of course, the ultimate goal should be to spend time with the ones you love, not simply to have more Facebook-worthy vacations.

The Two Most Dangerous Times In Your Life— Birth and Retirement

Dan Beuttner, a National Geographic Fellow, spent years traveling the world looking for the secrets to a long, healthy life. His eventual book, *Blue Zones*, summarizes his findings from small communities across four continents—Europe (Sardina, Italy; Ikaria, Greece), Asia (Okinawa, Japan), South/Central America (Nicoya, Costa Rica) and North America (Loma Linda, California).

In these "blue zones," Buettner and his team of researchers found much higher percentages of healthy adults living well into their late nineties and beyond one hundred.[12] What were their secrets? Plant-based diets, active lifestyles, strong community ties, and a deep sense of purpose seemed to be consistent themes.

Buettner gave a summary of his research in a September 2009 TED talk.* In his talk he suggests the two most dangerous times in a person's life are when they are born and when they retire. The first year of life is obviously a very risky time for all creatures, but why is retirement also fraught with risk? It turns out that many of the characteristics Buettner found in the blue zones fade away with retirement—daily physical activity, community ties, and a sense of purpose, to name a few.

If your identity is based on your income or your job title, then retirement can be a pretty big shock. You

---

* https://youtu.be/I-jk9ni4XWk

lose those work connections to people and your sense of purpose the moment your career ends. Buettner and his research team discovered one blue zone community on a small Japanese island that had a name for a life purpose—*ikigai*. The Japanese translation is "a sense of life worth living," and virtually all the centenarians Buettner talked to on the island could easily explain their personal ikigai. It was part of their culture.

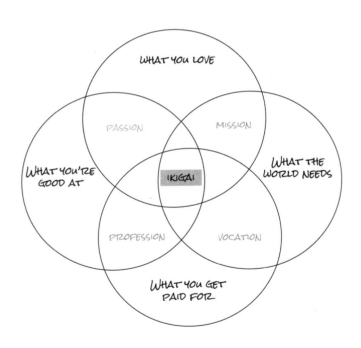

In a separate study of forty-three thousand Japanese adults, the participants with strongly expressed ikigai had significantly lower rates of death, particularly cardiovascular deaths, over the following seven years.[13] It's very important to note that ikigai is not derived from societies' definition of purpose—power, economic or social status—but rather it is cultivated internally, uniquely by each individual.

A 2006 paper from the National Bureau of Economic Research supports Buettner's contention that retirement is a particularly dangerous time in life. They found a strong connection between retirement and declining health. The incidence of illness increased, while mobility and mental wellness declined between 6 and 16 percent during the first few years after retirement.[14] These negative effects turned out to be stronger when a person's retirement was involuntary.

If you have developed deep, meaningful relationships throughout your life and beyond your career, then retirement can be just a turning point where you spend more time with friends and less time with (ex)coworkers. However, if your work has been allowed to consume your time and energy for decades, then retirement is not a turning point but rather a stopping point. In this case a person's physical and mental activity levels can drop dramatically in a short period of time.

In an upcoming paper, Professor Cowen surveys a number of reasons why many of us may enjoy working—from the obvious, like status and more money, to less obvious influences, such as social, psychological, and demographic factors. According to the paper, the hours worked per person has not changed much since World War II, in spite of large changes in technology and productivity, along with smaller positive growth in personal income. We should expect people to work less as their incomes and productivity increase, yet professor Cowen points out, "One of the big lessons of economic data is that people really like work."[15]

Happiness, as you can see, is complicated. We know that money doesn't necessarily make for a happy life; however, many factors, like social status and conspicuous consumption, are directly influenced by our income. We may continue to work just as hard as previous generations because of those external benefits, or, as Cowen suggests, we may enjoy working for a host of other reasons.

The question is, how can you best navigate the complicated journey of happiness? Here's what Ben Casnocha recommends—think of your success and happiness in terms of a dashboard instead of a leaderboard. A dashboard, like the one in your car, provides lots of information about your driving experience but tells you nothing about the cars around you. Your happiness can be measured in the same manner, i.e., relative to the internal conditions you control. A leaderboard, on the other hand, forces you onto that hedonic treadmill or status ladder. As Casnocha tells us in his article, "you should measure yourself in the spirit of improving upon your last best record, not what an opponent has accomplished. Leaderboards turn your attention to others; dashboards turn your attention within."[16]

HAPPINESS DASHBOARD

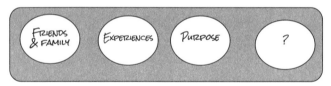

Over the years I've had clients who worked as practicing surgeons well into their late sixties and seventies. Earlier in the book I mentioned Peter Bernstein, an economic historian who wrote several of his most popular books well after he turned seventy. When I interviewed John Bogle in 2009, he had just turned eighty and was on his second heart transplant. At the time, he was busy working on a brief for a pending Supreme Court case, writing regular op-ed pieces for the major newspapers, and rewriting his classic book *Common Sense on Mutual Funds*. These people were not slowing down well into their seventies and eighties, and I believe it was due, in large part, to their happiness dashboard—their "ikigai."

Step four on your path to Wealthfulness is to intentionally discover your personal definition of happiness and meaning separate from status or money.

5

Money and Your Goals:
Ideas to Help You Take Action

"Knowing is not enough; we must apply.
Willing is not enough; we must do."
—*Johann Wolfgang von Goethe[1]*

You've made it this far on your path toward Wealthfulness, and we're closing in on the end. At this point I hope I've convinced you that your financial world requires some focused attention from time to time. I've also offered a simple, straightforward strategy for investing in chapter 2 that should free up your time, along with a range of mistakes to avoid in chapter 3. In chapter 4 I tried to expand the discussion by arguing that happiness is every bit as important as money when it comes to a meaningful life. That's what we're looking for, right? A meaningful life?

But it's all just talk unless you can break through the barriers that keep many families in a constant state of financial distress. You must start taking action. And that is where this chapter begins. Luckily, behavioral finance has also uncovered many ways to help us become more effective and productive.

Setting Goals Works

Research shows that setting your goals and writing them down improves your chances for success in achieving those goals—just the act of documenting them.[2] But setting goals and sticking to them can be hard work when faced with your daily distractions. It's easier, and far more natural, to allow that elephant in your head to meander through the jungle of decisions you face each day—directionless and motivated by immediate pain or pleasure. Unfortunately, it's unlikely that beast will stick to your plan or find the best path to reach your long-term goals.

Going through the exercise of creating a financial plan that contains both quantitative and qualitative goals will, without a doubt, help you realize a greater potential for yourself and your family. The planning process helps in several ways, both consciously and subconsciously, by:

120

1. Starting a dialog about the future between family members.
2. Establishing priorities.
3. Specifying your goals.
4. Uncovering forgotten or neglected issues.
5. Defining a plan of action.
6. Priming your subconscious to act toward your goals.

Voluntary Simplicity

"Everything should be made as simple as possible, but not simpler."[3]

—*Albert Einstein*

During the summer following the 2008 financial crisis I spent some time traveling around the country talking to people connected to the financial profession—authors, practitioners, elder statesmen, and academics. What had we just experienced? Had the crisis changed the financial world forever? What should we be doing differently?

On one of those trips I had lunch with a friend, Scott Burns, in Santa Fe, New Mexico. Scott has been a syndicated financial columnist for decades, dedicating much of his career to arguing for a simpler, low-cost approach to investing—a message of market return investing that is finally resonating with investors.

Over lunch I described a trend I had noticed among my neighbors and friends. In the wake of the financial crisis, they seemed to be focusing more on their families and relationships; people were downsizing their lifestyles with less stuff and fewer activities and were spending more time in the local community. Similar to the national response after 9/11, the financial crisis was bringing families and communities closer together in tangible ways, and I sensed we were better parents and friends for it.

Scott recommended a book, written more than thirty years earlier, that described the ideas and trends I was trying to understand. Duanne Elgin's book *Voluntary Simplicity* was published in 1981—just a few years after Watergate, the end of the Vietnam War, and the 73–74 recession. It was a time when citizens questioned the established political systems, feared global economic changes, and worried about their jobs and their children's futures. Looking back, it was a time that probably felt much like today for many people.

Here's how Elgin summarized the idea of voluntary simplicity:

With a lifestyle of conscious simplicity, we can seek our riches in caring families and friendships, reverence for nature, meaningful work, exuberant play, social contribution, collaboration across generation, local communities and creative arts. With conscious simplicity, we can seek lives that are rich with experiences, satisfaction, and learning rather than packed with things.[4]

Long before many of the concepts were formalized in psychology or economics, Elgin was describing ideas such as the *hedonic treadmill* and *choice overload*. He was also calling attention to many of the recipes for a long, happy life found in the blue zone research of Dan Buettner.

We face daunting complexity in every aspect of our lives in this digital age. I cannot foresee a time when things will become less complex or ever slow down. We can, however, make conscious choices for ourselves and our families to simplify and prioritize how we spend our time and money.

So, let's say you find the ideas of simplicity and valuing people over things appealing. Deciding to make some changes is relatively easy; staying on track, not so much. This is where a Wealthfulness mind-set comes into play.

Economics is teeming with new research in an area called *motivated beliefs*.

Motivation, it seems, helps explain many of the ideas in behavioral finance and happiness research we've covered in the previous chapters. More importantly for this discussion, however, motivation also gives us some useful tools that encourage positive behavior and better outcomes. Psychologist/economist Daniel Ariely has written an excellent book on the subject, *Payoff: The Hidden Logic That Shapes Our Motivations*. Here's how he sees the possibility of motivation:

> To motivate ourselves and others successfully, we need to provide a sense of connection and meaning—remembering that meaning is not always synonymous with personal happiness. Arguably, the most powerful motivator in the world is our connection to others.[5]

The purpose of a written financial plan is to discover that connection and meaning Professor Ariely describes. The plan will connect your sacrifices now—working, saving, and budgeting—to your future goals and dreams. Again, we are reminded that it is not the material items or short-term pleasures but the people and experiences that matter.

Nudge—The Art and Science of Getting Better Decisions

Sometimes motivation may not be enough to keep you on track. Luckily, there are other behavioral tools at your disposal. Before we dive into the next area of behavioral finance, let me share with you a few random facts you may or may not know:

1. If you use a smaller plate, you'll eat less.
2. Kids eat more fruit when it is put at the front of the cafeteria line.
3. New employees save much more in their 401(k) accounts if they are enrolled automatically.
4. In Sweden 85.4 percent of the population are organ donors. Next door in Denmark only 4.25 percent of the population elect to be organ donors.

What do these factoids have in common? They all include what economists Cass Sundstein and Richard Thaler call a "nudge."[6]

Presentation matters. It's a timeless truth that parents, politicians, and con artists have known for millennia. How a set of choices is presented can significantly influence the ultimate decisions people make. Psychologists call it framing—setting up a situation in a way that encourages a particular outcome.

Thanks to Sundstein and Thaler, more 401(k) plans are building automatic savings options into the choices, where employees can sign up for escalating percentages of their pay going to savings each year. Some plans are now automatically enrolling new employees at a minimum level of savings, rather than starting them at zero and requiring their action to start saving. It's called "opting in," and setting the default for new employees to be automatically opted in, rather than opted out, can make a huge difference in 401(k) participation. In turn, higher participation and higher savings rates can make a significant impact on long-term retirement prospects for those employees.

Let's go back to the facts I mentioned earlier. Why is organ donation so vastly different between the neighboring countries of Denmark and Sweden? On the surface, it would seem they have much in common—culture, language origins, weather, political and economic environments. Why the difference in organ donation?

The answer, it seems, is how the question of organ donation is "framed" in each country. In Denmark, citizens are automatically nondonors unless they choose to "opt in" to the program. In Sweden citizens are automatically organ donors unless they "opt out." That subtle difference between the two countries accounts for virtually all the difference between donor rates of 85 percent and 5 percent.

It's important to note that opting in in Denmark or opting out in Sweden takes almost no effort. It's often no more than checking a box in either case, but the difference is profound. Citizens in either case get to keep all their rights and options—no one is forced to donate or kept from donating, and yet a simple nudge can lead to improved outcomes for everyone.

You can use nudges in your own life to encourage financial responsibility and stewardship. You can find some effective "nudges" on my website, www.Wealthfulness.com. There I keep an updated list of useful tools to help you increase your savings, fix that leaky budget, or find a host of other ideas to get your personal finances in order.

Feedback Loops—How Information Helps Us Make Better Decisions

Have you ever wondered about the speed limit signs you often see in school zones—the ones with a digital display showing you how fast you're going? Does that really seem necessary? You probably already know your speed.

The strange thing is those signs work. They are very effective at keeping you within the posted speed limits. One study found that dynamic speed displays (as they are called) can reduce the speed in school zones by up to nine miles per hour.[7] That's an amazing result when you consider a typical legal school zone speed is only twenty miles per hour. But, as Thomas Goetz asks in his 2011 article for *Wired* magazine, why is it that "giving speeders redundant information with no consequence would somehow compel them to do something few of us are inclined to do: slow down?"[8]

Those signs work because they create a feedback loop to help you make instantaneous decisions about your behavior. It's not likely that most of us speed through school zones on purpose; no, it's much more likely that we just haven't processed the idea yet that our car is traveling too fast. That flashing sign places your speed at the front of the cue for your attention.

We now have watches, phones, and refrigerator doors that can provide feedback to us—virtually anything you want to place at the front of your attention cue can be tracked and reported. Likewise, there are phone apps and websites to help you track your financial life; budgeting, saving, portfolio, credit score, etc. These tools can be harnessed to help you improve your financial picture across many dimensions.

Nowadays there is no excuse if you are motivated to work on your finances. But don't get lost in the noise. Feedback tools are only useful insofar as they improve your decision making and increase your mental bandwidth. Conversely, if you become paralyzed with data or consumed by the tools, you're better off without them. There is a medical word for that condition—iatrogenic, where the cure is worse than the original disease.[9] Sadly, much of the financial industry is dominated by products, tools, and information that can be just as harmful as doing nothing at all.

Take the well-known research tools from Morningstar, for instance. For years we've known that a simple search for low-cost funds will generally give you better mutual fund recommendations than their famous five-star ratings.[10] If you dig deeper into the Morningstar database, past the star ratings, you will find an absolute treasure trove of data on just about every possible mutual fund, ETF, or stock in the United States. You can find rankings against similar funds, bull versus bear market performance, after-tax comparisons, sector breakdowns, and on, and on, and on.

Very quickly that kind of data will lead you directly to the old problem of choice conflict. There are more than eight thousand distinct mutual funds in the Morningstar database, along with another two thousand ETFs and twenty thousand individual stocks. Before you rush down that rabbit hole, remind yourself of your new mind-set— simple, low-cost investing that rarely needs your attention once it's done correctly. Do not waste your valuable time.

As the financial industry jockeys for your attention and your pocketbook, it will not be rushing to provide you with simple, uncomplicated solutions to save you money. The industry behemoths will continue to overwhelm you with more information, more complicated products, and more tools for trading and researching. Don't do it. If you're not spending more quality time with your friends and family, and if you don't feel more confident about your finances, the tools aren't working.

Step five of the Wealthfulness mind-set is to use tools from behavioral finance to become more effective in achieving your goals.

Conclusion

My hope is that this book has introduced you to a few new ideas that can dramatically impact your financial future. Whether you are already in retirement, planning for when that day will come, or just starting your career, the ideas we've covered in this book can improve your life.

Do you remember Claire's story from an earlier chapter? She had lost her faith in investing but regained it over time with patience and a well-thought-out financial plan. Not long ago she sent me an e-mail after reading a draft of this book. Here's what it said: "I've learned that successful investing is a long-term approach, not a fast dash to the finish line. It's so important for people to start early with their financial planning. I hope my bad experiences over all those years will help others not make the same mistakes I did."

That is really all you need to know.

Wealthfulnesss is both an awareness of your current financial situation and an attitude about how you will influence your future—give your financial plan the attention it deserves; simplify your investments; understand your emotional attachment to money and the psychological biases that can mislead you; foster a sense of purpose in your life that coincides with your personal definition of happiness; and then, finally, take a few simple steps to put yourself in a position to succeed. Nothing I've asked you to do in this book is even slightly difficult, with the possible exception of letting go of your ego and a few outdated preconceptions about the world of finance.

Good luck.

Recommended Reading

Investing—Classics

- William Bernstein, *The Four Pillars of Investing: Lessons for Building a Winning Portfolio* (USA: McGraw-Hill Companies, Inc., 2002).

- John Bogle, *Bogle On Mutual Funds: New Perspectives For The Intelligent Investor* (New Jersey: Wiley Investment Classics, 2015).

- Charles Ellis, *Winning the Loser's Game: Timeless Strategies for Successful Investing* (New York: McGraw-Hill Education, 2017).

- Burton G. Malkiel, *A Random Walk Down Wall Street: The Time-Tested Strategy for Successful Investing*, 11th edition (New York: W. W. Norton & Company, 2014).

Behavioral Finance

- George A. Akerloff and Robert J. Shiller, *Animal Spirits: How Human Psychology Drives The Economy, And Why It Matters For Global Capitalism* (Princeton: Princeton University Press, 2009).

- Robert H. Frank, *Falling Behind: How Rising Inequality Harms the Middle Class* (University of California Press, 2013).

- Daniel Kahneman, *Thinking, Fast and Slow* (New York: Farrar, Straus and Giroux, 2015), Kindle edition.

- Sendhil Mullainathan and Eldar Shafir. *Scarcity: Why Having Too Little Means So Much* (New York: Times Books, Henry Holt and Company, 2013).

- Barry Schwarz, *Paradox of Choice: Why More is Less* (New York: HarperCollins, 2005).

- Richard H. Thaler and Cass R. Sunstein, *Nudge: Improving Decisions about Health, Wealth, and Happiness* (London: Penguin Books, 2009).

Psychology & Happiness

- Dan Ariely, *Payoff: The Hidden Logic That Shapes Our Motivations,* TED Books (New York: TED Books, Simon & Schuster, 2016), Kindle edition.

- Dan Beuttner, *The Blue Zones: Lessons for Living Longer from the People Who've Lived the Longest*, reprint edition (National Geographic, 2010).

- Judson Brewer, *The Craving Mind: From Cigarettes to*

Smartphones to Love—Why We Get Hooked and How We Can Break Bad Habits (Yale University Press, 2017), Kindle edition.

- Duane Elgin, *Voluntary Simplicity: Toward a Way of Life That Is Outwardly Simple, Inwardly Rich*, 2nd ed. (New York: HarperCollins, 2010).

- Goleman, *Focus: The Hidden Driver of Excellence* (New York: HarperCollins, 2013).

- Carol Graham, *Happiness Around the World: The Paradox of Happy Peasants and Miserable Millionaires* (New York: Oxford University Press, 2009).

- Jonathan Haidt, *The Happiness Hypothesis: Finding Modern Truth in Ancient Wisdom* (New York: Basic Books, 2006), Kindle edition.

- Amit Sood, *The Mayo Clinic Guide to Stress-Free Living* (Cambridge, MA: Da Capo Press/Lifelong Books, 2013), Kindle edition.

Economics

- Peter L. Bernstein, *Against the Gods: The Remarkable Story of Risk* (New York: John Wiley & Sons, Inc., 1998), Kindle edition.

- Tyler Cowen, *The Complacent Class: The Self-Defeating*

Quest For The American Dream (New York: St. Martin's Press, 2017).

- Laurence J. Kotlikoff and Scott Burns, *Spend 'til the End: Raising Your Living Standard in Today's Economy and When You Retire* (New York: Simon & Schuster, 2010).

Notes

Preface

1. Atul Gawande, "The Heroism of Incremental Care," *New Yorker*, January 23, 2017, http://www.newyorker.com/magazine/2017/01/23/theheroism-of-incremental-care.html.

Introduction

1. Sendhil Mullainathan and Eldar Shafir, *Scarcity: Why Having Too Little Means So Much* (New York: Times Books, Henry Holt and Company, 2013), Kindle edition, 52–53.

2. Annamaria Lusardi and Olivia S. Mitchell, "Financial Literacy and Planning: Implications for Retirement Wellbeing," 2011. 16–17. doi: 10.3386/w17078.

3. Laura Shin, "The Retirement Crisis: Why 68% Of Americans Aren't Saving In An Employer-Sponsored Plan," *Forbes*, October 12, 2015, https://www.forbes.com/sites/laurashin/2015/04/09/the-retirement-crisis-why-68-of-americans-arent-saving-in-an-

employer-sponsored-plan/#3212985a2152.

4. Laurence J. Kotlikoff and Scott Burns, *Spend 'til the End: Raising Your Living Standard in Today's Economy and When You Retire* (New York: Simon & Schuster, 2010), 55.

5. Jamie Gonzalez, "Credit Card Ownership Statistics," CreditCards.com, February 2, 2016, http://www. creditcards.com/credit-card-news/ownership-statistics.php.

6. "NerdWallet's 2016 Household Debt Study," NerdWallet, accessed May 5, 2016, https://www. nerdwallet.com/blog/average-credit-card-debt-household/.

7. Maria Lamagna, "Americans are now in more debt than they were before the financial crisis," Marketwatch, December 23, 2016, http://www.marketwatch.com/ story/this-is-how-much-credit-card-debt-americans-racked-up-in-2016-2016-12-20.

8. Jessica Dickler, "66 million Americans have no emergency savings," CNBC, June 21, 2016, http:// www.cnbc.com/2016/06/21/66-million-americans-have-no-emergency-savings.html.

9. Limra, "LIMRA: Nearly 5 Million More U.S. Households Have Life Insurance Coverage,"

PR Newswire: news distribution, targeting and monitoring, September 29, 2016, http://www.prnewswire.com/news-releases/limra--nearly-5-million-more-us-households-have-life-insurance-coverage-300335782.html.

10. Jesse Bricker, Lisa J. Dettling, Alice Henriques, Joanne W. Hsu, Kevin B. Moore, John Sabelhaus, Jeffrey Thompson, and Richard A. Windle, "Changes in U.S. Family Finances from 2010 to 2013: Evidence from the Survey of Consumer Finances," Federal Reserve Bulletin (September 2014), pp. 1–40.

11. "Stress in America: 2013," American Psychological Association, February 11, 2014, http://www.apa.org/news/press/releases/stress/2013/highlights.aspx.

12. Steven Covey, *7 Habits of Highly Effective People* (Salt Lake City: Franklin Covey, 2002).

Chapter 1

1. Anthony DeCurtis, *In Other Words: Artists Talk About Life and Work* (Wisconsin: Hal Leonard Publishing Co, 2005), p. 267.

2. Amit Sood, *The Mayo Clinic Guide to Stress-Free Living*

(Cambridge, MA: Da Capo Press/Lifelong Books, 2013), Kindle edition, 155.

3. Sood, *The Mayo Clinic Guide,* Preface.

4. Jonathan Haidt, *The Happiness Hypothesis: Finding Modern Truth in Ancient Wisdom* (New York: Basic Books, 2006), Kindle edition, introduction.

5. "Stress in America: Paying with our health," *American Psychological Association*, February 4, 2015, http://www.apa.org/news/press/releases/stress/2014/financial-stress.aspx.

6. Robert Wood Johnson Foundation and Harvard School, "The Burden of Stress in America," RWJF, December 19, 2016, http://www.rwjf.org/en/library/research/2014/07/the-burden-of-stress-in-america.html.

7. Judson Brewer, *The Craving Mind: From Cigarettes to Smartphones to Love—Why We Get Hooked and How We Can Break Bad Habits* (Yale University Press, 2017), Kindle edition, 29.

8. Daniel Goleman, *Focus: The Hidden Driver of Excellence* (New York: HarperCollins), 10.

9. Jeffrey C. Ely, "Kludged," *American Economic Journal*: Microeconomics 3, no. 3 (2011): 210–31, doi:10.1257/mic.3.3.210.

Chapter 2

1. John Bogle, *The Clash of the Cultures: Investment vs. Speculation* (New Jersey: John Wiley & Sons, Inc., 2012).

2. James B. Stewart, "Hedge Funds Lose Calpers, and More," *New York Times*, September 26, 2014, accessed April 13, 2017, https://www.nytimes.com/2014/09/27/business/in-calperss-departure-a-watershed-moment-for-hedge-funds.html?_r=0.

3. Diane Del Guercio and Jonathan Reuter, "Mutual Fund Performance and the Incentive to Generate Alpha," NBER, October 2011, http://www.nber.org/papers/w17491, 4.

4. Sendhil Mullainathan, Markus Noeth, and Antoinette Schoar, "The Market for Financial Advice: An Audit Study," NBER, March 2012, http://www.nber.org/papers/w17929.

5. Charles Ellis, *Winning the Loser's Game: Timeless Strategies for Successful Investing* (New York: McGraw-Hill Education, 2017).

6. Mullainathan, Noeth, and Schoar, "The Market for Financial Advice," 1.

7. Jane Bryant Quinn, interviewed by Lance Alston and

Jim Whiddon, April 4, 2008.

Chapter 3

1. Warren E. Buffett, "Buy American. I Am.," *New York Times*, October 16, 2008, accessed April 13, 2017, http://www.nytimes.com/2008/10/17/opinion/17buffett.html.

2. Daniel Kahneman, *Thinking, Fast and Slow* (New York: Farrar, Straus and Giroux, 2015), Kindle edition, 283.

3. Daniel Kahneman, Barbara L. Fredrickson, Charles A. Schreiber, and Donald A. Redelmeier, "When More Pain Is Preferred to Less: Adding a Better End," *Psychological Science* 4, no. 6 (1993): 401–05. http://www.jstor.org/stable/40062570.

4. Ronald J. Baker, *Implementing Value Pricing: A Radical Business Model for Professional Firms* (Hoboken, NJ: Wiley, 2010), 45.

5. "Noticeboard," CCP Research Foundation: Noticeboard, February 18, 2016, http://www.ccpresearchfoundation.com/noticeboard?item=30279-video-the-cost-of-trust-gone-wrong-300-billion-and-counting.

6. JPMorgan Chase & Co (2015), 2015 Annual Report,

57.

7. Bank of America Corporation (2015), 2015 Annual Report, 5.

8. Paola Sapienza and Luigi Zingales, "Financial Trust Index," Financial Trust Index, accessed May 9, 2016, http://www.financialtrustindex.org/.

9. Sapienza and Zingales, "Financial Trust Index," http://www.financialtrustindex.org/.

10. "US Financial Services Industry Digital Ad Spend Passes $7 Billion," EMarketer, May 21, 2015, accessed May 9, 2016, https://www.emarketer.com/Article/US-Financial-Services-Industry-Digital-Ad-Spend-Passes-7-Billion/1012508.

11. B.M. Barber and T. Odean, "Boys will be Boys: Gender, Overconfidence, and Common Stock Investment," *The Quarterly Journal of Economics* 116, no. 1 (2001): 261–92, doi:10.1162/003355301556400. T. Odean, interviewed by Lance Alston, 2015.

12. P. Sapienza, L. Zingales, and D. Maestripieri, "Gender differences in financial risk aversion and career choices are affected by testosterone," *Proceedings of the National Academy of Sciences* 106, no. 36 (2009): 15268–5273, doi:10.1073/pnas.0907352106.

13. Peter L. Bernstein, *Against the Gods: The Remarkable*

Story of Risk (New York: John Wiley & Sons, Inc., 1998), Kindle edition, introduction.

14. Shane Frederick, George Loewenstein, and Ted O'Donoghue, "Time Discounting and Time Preference: A Critical Review," *Journal of Economic Literature* 40, no. 2 (2002): 351–401, doi:10.1257/002205102320161311.

15. Daniel Kahneman, *Thinking, Fast and Slow* (New York: Farrar, Straus and Giroux, 2015), Kindle edition, 283.

16. "Variable Annuities: What You Should Know," US Securities and Exchange Commission, April 18, 2011, https://www.sec.gov/reportspubs/investor-publications/investorpubsvaranntyhtm.html.

Chapter 4

1. Benjamin Franklin, BrainyQuote.com, Xplore Inc, 2017, accessed April 13, 2917, https://www.brainyquote.com/quotes/quotes/b/benjaminfr165453.html.

2. "Happy Ambition: Success, Status Cocaine, and Happiness," Ben Casnocha, June 10, 2016, http://casnocha.com/happy-ambition-status-cocaine.

3. D. Kahneman and A. Deaton, "High income

improves evaluation of life but not emotional well-being," *Proceedings of the National Academy of Sciences* 107, no. 38 (2010): 16489–6493, doi:10.1073/pnas.1011492107.

To be completely fair, increases in income up to around $120,000 seem to continue increasing how you report feeling about your life, but emotionally you're no better off.

4. Martin E. P. Seligman, *Authentic Happiness: Using the New Positive Psychology to Realize Your Potential for Lasting Fulfillment* (Simon and Schuster, 2002).

5. Carol Graham, *The Pursuit of Happiness: An Economy of Well-Being* (Washington, DC: Brookings Institution Press, 2012).

6. Barry Schwarz, *Paradox of Choice: Why More is Less* (New York: HarperCollins, 2005).

7. Haidt, *The Happiness Hypothesis*, 101.

8. Lee Eisenberg, *The Number: What Do You Need for the Rest of Your Life and What Will It Cost?*, reprint edition (Free Press, 2006). Interviewed by Lance Alston & Jim Whiddon, January 6, 2006.

9. Carol Graham, *Happiness Around the World: The Paradox of Happy Peasants and Miserable Millionaires* (New York: Oxford University Press, 2009), 213.

10. Robert H. Frank, *Falling Behind: How Rising Inequality Harms the Middle Class* (University of California Press, 2013).

The idea of conspicuous consumption can be traced back to Thorsten Veblen in the nineteenth century.

11. "Why hasn't economic progress lowered work hours more? Tyler Cowen, Hayek Lecture Series," YouTube video, 41:41, filmed March 2016, posted by "Duke University Department of Political Science," March 31, 2016, https://youtu.be/8Pk654J8-5c.

12. Dan Beuttner, *The Blue Zones: Lessons for Living Longer from the People Who've Lived the Longest*, reprint edition (National Geographic, 2010).

13. Toshimasa Sone, Naoki Nakaya, Kaori Ohmori, Taichi Shimazu, Mizuka Higashiguchi, Masako Kakizaki, Nobutaka Kikuchi, Shinichi Kuriyama, and Ichiro Tsuji. "Sense of life worth living (ikigai) and mortality in Japan: Ohsaki Study." *Psychosomatic Medicine* 70, no. 6 (2008): 709–715.

14. Dhaval Dave, Inas Rashad, and Jasmina Spasojevic, "The Effects of Retirement on Physical and Mental Health Outcomes," *Southern Economic Journal, Southern Economic Association* 75, no. 2 (October

2008): 497–523, doi:10.3386/w12123.

15. Tyler Cowen, "Why Hasn't Economic Progress Lowered Work Hours More?," working paper, June 3, 2016.

16. "Happy Ambition: Success, Status Cocaine, and Happiness," Ben Casnocha, June 10, 2016, http://casnocha.com/happy-ambition-status-cocaine.

Chapter 5

1. Johann Wolfgang von Goethe, BrainyQuote. com, Xplore Inc, 2017, accessed April 10, 2017, https://www.brainyquote.com/quotes/quotes/j/johannwolf161315.html.

2. S. Turkay, "Setting Goals: Who, Why, How?," Harvard Office of the Vice Provost for Advances in Learning, 2014, http://vpal.harvard.edu/publications/setting-goals-who-why-how.

3. Alice Calaprice, *The Ultimate Quotable Einstein* (Princeton, New Jersey, Princeton University Press, 2011), 475.

4. Duane Elgin, *Voluntary Simplicity: Toward a Way of Life That Is Outwardly Simple, Inwardly Rich*, 2nd ed. (New York: HarperCollins, 2010), 17–18.

5. Dan Ariely, *Payoff: The Hidden Logic That Shapes Our Motivations*, TED Books (New York: TED Books, Simon & Schuster, 2016), Kindle edition, Loc 1088.

6. Richard H. Thaler and Cass R. Sunstein, *Nudge: Improving Decisions about Health, Wealth, and Happiness* (London: Penguin Books, 2009).

7. Gerald Ullman and Elisabeth Rose, "Evaluation of Dynamic Speed Display Signs," *Transportation Research Record: Journal of the Transportation Research Board* 1918 (2005): 92–97, doi:10.3141/1918-12.

8. Thomas Goetz, "Harnessing the Power of Feedback Loops," *Wired*, July 2011.

9. Scott Burns, "Is Investing Really Like Brain Surgery?," AssetBuilder Knowledge Center, May 23, 2014, https://assetbuilder.com/knowledge-center/articles/scott-burns/is_investing_really_like_brain_surgery.

10. Russel Kinnel, "How Expense Ratios and Star Ratings Predict Success," Morningstar Articles RSS, August 9, 2010, accessed May 9, 2016, http://news.morningstar.com/articlenet/article.aspx?id=347327.

About the Author

Lance Alston is founder and president of New Dimensions Wealth Management, LLC, in Allen, Texas. He holds a master's degree in economics from George Mason University, a bachelor's degree in international business from the University of Texas (Austin), and is a CERTIFIED FINANCIAL PLANNER™ professional. As the cohost of a personal finance podcast, he has interviewed a wide range of guests from the areas of economics, finance, and public policy: best-selling authors; members of the Cabinet, Federal Reserve, and Congress; and a handful of Nobel laureates in economics.

During his nineteen-year career, Lance has personally helped more than five hundred families create personalized financial plans tailored to their specific needs and goals. Those experiences have taught him a few important lessons: uncomplicated solutions are usually best, investing costs are very important, and money isn't everything.

Lance lives in McKinney, Texas, with his two daughters, Claire and Olivia. When he isn't helping his clients plan for their future, Lance enjoys traveling with his girls, who are his favorite travel companions.